"This is an exciting and instructionally directional book about the most challenging, strategically most potent and yet largely neglected mission field—the university classrooms of our globally interconnected and yet religiously and culturally diverse world. From the wealth of their pedagogical wisdom, plethora of their crosscultural experiences and the depth of their kingdom commitments, the authors persuasively argue and richly illustrate how important knowing is for going and understanding is for teaching. My advice to all who are missional in their international teaching: this book must be read before going and taken along for self-evaluating reference."

DR. PETER KUZMIČ, *Eva B. and Paul E. Toms Distinguished Professor of World Missions and European Studies, Gordon-Conwell Theological Seminary, and founding president, Evangelical Theological Seminary, Osijek, Croatia*

"There are few people who are qualified to write a book like this. And there are few books that inform, challenge, persuade and entertain like this does. Mike Romanowski and Teri McCarthy have delved deep and produced a stimulating and essential text for those called to Christian teaching across the globe. Don't leave home without it!"

ELAINE STORKEY, *president, Tearfund; Director of Training and Education, the Church of England Church Army*

"As president of a Christian college I very strongly recommend *Teaching in a Distant Classroom* to students interested in international missions (teaching or otherwise) and to all Christian faculty members in the U.S. Romanowski and McCarthy provide practical insights and heartwarming narratives that will help students decide whether teaching abroad is for them and, if so, help them prepare to do so well. All faculty members should read it because it will help them think through what it means to be a Christian who teaches. This book, which could actually be called a survival guide, is invaluable for students who sense God's call to teach overseas as a Christian missionary and for faculty who find themselves increasingly confronting diverse and conflicting worldviews in U.S. classrooms. It should be on every Christian campus in the nation."

DAN STRUBLE, PH.D., *president, Montreat College*

"I sure wish I could have read this book before I began teaching in Nigeria. It's better to learn from its authors than from Hard Knocks University!"

CHUCK WHITE, PH.D., *Professor of Christian Thought and History, Spring Arbor University, and Visiting Professor, University of Jos, Nigeria*

"There is no other book quite like *Teaching in a Distant Classroom*. For years I've been mobilizing young people and retirees to go overseas and teach. I wish I could have put this book in the hands of every one of those young people and retirees that I've mobilized! The book is brutally honest about integrity issues as well as other problems likely to be encountered. While it gives great 'how-to' advice for flourishing in a crosscultural situation, it also deals with foundational questions like pedagogy, philosophy and worldview."

HOWARD CULBERTSON, D.MIN., *professor of missions,*
Southern Nazarene University

"*Teaching in a Distant Classroom* is a valuable introduction to college teaching as crosscultural ministry. Indeed, as a former college provost who cares a great deal about teaching Christianly, I think that it could be valuable for college teachers anywhere, including Christian colleges in the United States! These days, all college teaching is 'crosscultural ministry.' It is remarkable how little guidance newly minted Ph.D.s have received in the art and craft of good teaching, even if they have some university teaching experience. This book offers valuable introductions to these topics, and much more, including the life of learning as a genuine calling from God, the cultural assumptions behind much of Western college teaching and what it means to be an authentic ambassador of Jesus Christ in all of one's life. This is a wise and practical book, and I hope that many Christian professors will read it."

JOEL CARPENTER, PH.D., *director, Nagel Institute for the*
Study of World Christianity

"Written from passionate hearts aflame for Christ and his kingdom, *Teaching in a Distant Classroom* is the most authentic, relevant and inspirational professional guide available today for those considering teaching abroad. An inspirational challenge and complete resource for all who teach, this book should be required reading for all Christian college students considering teaching overseas."

STEPHEN D. LIVESAY, PH.D., *president, Bryan College*

TEACHING IN A
DISTANT CLASSROOM

Crossing Borders for
Global Transformation

MICHAEL H. ROMANOWSKI
AND TERI McCARTHY

IVP Books
An imprint of InterVarsity Press
Downers Grove, Illinois

InterVarsity Press
P.O. Box 1400, Downers Grove, IL 60515-1426
World Wide Web: www.ivpress.com
E-mail: email@ivpress.com

InterVarsity Press® is the book-publishing division of InterVarsity Christian Fellowship/USA®, a student movement active on campus at hundreds of universities, colleges and schools of nursing in the United States of America, and a member movement of the International Fellowship of Evangelical Students. For information about local and regional activities, write Public Relations Dept., InterVarsity Christian Fellowship/USA, 6400 Schroeder Rd., P.O. Box 7895, Madison, WI 53707-7895, or visit the IVCF website at <www.intervarsity.org>.

All Scripture quotations, unless otherwise indicated, are taken from the Holy Bible, Today's New International Version™ Copyright © 2001 by International Bible Society. All rights reserved.

Figure 4 on page 130 is copyright, CAST. Used by permission.

While all stories in this book are true, some names and identifying details have been changed to protect the privacy of those involved. Sidebar stories are used with permission.

Design: Cindy Kiple
Images: flattened world globe: Digital Vision
          large classroom: Lisa Klumpp/iStockphoto
          Oxford University, England: Charlie Waite/Getty Images

ISBN 978-0-8308-3743-4

Printed in the United States of America ∞

Library of Congress Cataloging-in-Publication Data

Romanowski, Michael H., 1960-
  Teaching in a distant classroom: crossing borders for global
transformation / Michael H. Romanowski and Teri McCarthy.
        p. cm.
  Includes bibliographical references and index.
  ISBN 978-0-8308-3743-4 (pbk.: alk. paper)
  1. Missions—Educational work 2. Education (Christian theology) I.
McCarthy, Teri, 1959- II. Title.
BV2630.R66 2009
266'.02302437—dc22

2009031647

P	22	21	20	19	18	17	16	15	14	13	12	11	10	9	8	7	6	5	4	3	2	1
Y	27	26	25	24	23	22	21	20	19	18	17	16	15	14	13	12	11	10	09			

Contents

Introduction

Crossing borders to teach in a distant classroom can be the most surprising, challenging, difficult and rewarding experience life has to offer. However, even the most experienced teacher can be knocked off her feet by the hardships that come from living in a different culture. People who take teaching assignments overseas often underestimate these difficulties. As a result, they struggle both inside and outside the classroom.

The opportunity to live and teach abroad is sometimes idealized. Among Christians, the thought of serving Christ in a foreign land can seem noble and romantic. However, expatriates can be blindsided by the challenges of living and teaching crossculturally. Simple tasks such as ordering dinner in a local restaurant or making copies for a class assignment can become nightmares in a crosscultural situation. Anyone living and teaching overseas quickly discovers that norms of social discourse, manners, customs and daily life are gone. The honeymoon evaporates all too soon. Day-to-day difficulties and struggles can become overwhelming. In overseas classrooms, crosscultural challenges create conflicts and misunderstandings that not only can reduce the credibility of the foreign teacher but seriously hamper learning and create frustration for both teacher and student.

Classroom assumptions about learning and teaching that apply in the teacher's home culture don't necessarily transfer. Crosscultural teaching requires a committed individual who is well-prepared, reflective and most importantly, teachable. Misguided motives, combined with a lack of crosscultural understanding and preparedness, can cause even the most seasoned educator to crash and burn overseas.

Overseas teaching assignments require crosscultural sensitivity and self-understanding. The teacher in a distant land is like an athlete preparing for a game: practicing, knowing his own strengths and weaknesses, understanding the rules of the game and the layout of the field. Educators must understand their own cultural backgrounds and their personal limitations. This demands analysis of teaching strategies and understanding the host culture and its students' particular view of the world before classes even begin.

We have identified three common types of Christians teaching overseas. The first is the *seasoned veteran educator* with an extensive teaching background in North America. This person is an expert in her academic discipline, has a wide range of classroom experiences, and possesses a clear, well-formed philosophy of education and methodology, yet has no (or very limited) overseas exposure.

The second type is the professional expert. We call this the *sink-or-swim instructor*. They are not trained teachers, but perhaps experts in their fields. Many learned their teaching methods as graduate students. Some may be college-level instructors, while others became successful in their vocations and now want to teach overseas. However, North Americans are not innately equipped to teach internationally simply because they have a graduate degree or marketplace experience. Success in the overseas classroom is not guaranteed by North American know-how. Most of these well-meaning instructors find that teaching in North America and teaching overseas are two very different experiences.

Finally, there is the *recent college grad*. These are the most common, especially in Southeast Asia. These are enthusiastic, gung-ho followers of Christ who have earned their college degrees, signed up with a missions-sending organization, received the blessing of families and churches, and left home earnestly desiring to change the world for Jesus Christ. Unfortunately, good intentions don't necessarily lead to good teaching. The recent college grad brings energy and enthusiasm into the overseas classroom but few have any teaching skills, understanding of pedagogy, educational philosophy or even the basic skills needed to design a course syllabus. Even those who have some experience or formal teacher-training may lack the necessary insight, knowledge and understanding required to teach effectively in a crosscultural setting.

For the seasoned veteran educator, this book offers some guidelines for developing a fully orbed Christian worldview. It aims to shed light on the importance of excellence in the classroom and in relationships with students and faculty. Our goal is to help the seasoned veteran educator better understand teaching overseas as a true Christian mission, with Christ's lordship over all things.

For the sink-or-swim instructor, this text will help you form a philosophy of education and develop a pedagogical style. Our goal is to provide a starting point for shaping and focusing existing beliefs about the crosscultural classroom and for developing a more comprehensive Christian philosophy of education.

Finally, for the recent college grad, this text will encourage your reflection about experiences in education and help develop a working philosophy of education for teaching in a crosscultural environment. It will also help you consider how faith shapes your teaching and how teaching is a true Christian mission and calling.

This text is also designed to help the inexperienced *English as a Foreign Language (EFL) instructor*. Foreign universities are often willing to accept native English speakers holding a bachelor's degree (in any subject) to teach EFL courses. This need for EFL instructors is God's opportunity for believers to serve Christ in nations that are closed to traditional missionaries and Christian workers. Many such EFL teachers have their hearts in the right place, but the majority have little professional training or teaching experience. They may have taught Sunday school or Vacation Bible School or given professional presentations in the workplace, but these are not adequate preparation for teaching in an overseas classroom. Some missions organizations provide a six-week EFL intensive training course, but this is often still insufficient. This book is offered as a vital resource and training manual to equip instructors in grappling with the complexities of teaching in preparation to teach in a distant EFL classroom.

Because we are evangelical Christians, our concerns reach beyond pedagogy and academic discipline to include a strong commitment to the spiritual lives of our students and colleagues. This book is especially for other evangelical Christians who find themselves called to teach outside their homelands, taking seriously the words of Matthew 28:19-20:

> Go ye therefore, and teach all nations, baptizing them in the name of the Father, and of the Son and of the Holy Ghost: Teaching them to observe all things whatsoever I have commanded you: and, lo, I am with you always, even unto the end of the world. Amen. (KJV)

Most biblical scholars would agree that not all Christians are called to be formal evangelists. But certainly every Christian has gifts and abilities that can be tools to fulfill the Great Commission. Individuals with the ability to teach can further God's kingdom and reach the lost in nations with little or no Christian witness. As followers of Christ who teach, we can enter distant classrooms with well-honed teaching skills, excellent pedagogy, and a well-defined philosophy of education with a comprehensive Christian worldview. By doing so, we bring glory to God and Jesus Christ in classrooms around the world.

Whether you are a new or seasoned teacher, we hope this book will challenge you to think Christianly about your pedagogy. We will provide opportunities to engage in critical evaluation of the beliefs and values that are foundational for educational practices. Our goal is to spark reflection on educational theories and to differentiate between Christian and secular thinking about education and classroom teaching. We hope that you will be better prepared to present Christ within your academic discipline in a manner that is philosophically sound, practical and intellectually viable.

Real-life examples and stories are provided to illustrate principles and to emphasize the importance of critical reflection in the foreign classroom. As authors, we understand the limitations of any writing. So we include sections at the end of each chapter titled "Going Deeper, Going Further" that provide additional questions, exercises and recommended readings for further study.

This book is based on our international, crosscultural and personal teaching experiences in nearly a dozen nations. We have worked together on an academic training project in Kabul, Afghanistan. We have witnessed firsthand the good work Christian teachers have done around the globe. But we have also seen Christian teachers who have struggled and felt ill-equipped for their task. It is our hope and desire that this book can empower and equip our brothers and sisters in Christ who have dedicated their lives to teach for him in a distant classroom. We hope you will develop a Christian mind, thinking Christianly and critically about living and teaching as you bring the hope, life and light of Christ to students and colleagues abroad.

1

Agent 007

The Undercover
Christian Teacher

Often when Christians decide to go outside their homeland to teach—especially to creative-access or missionary-restricted countries—family and friends ask, "If you can't talk about Jesus in the classroom over there, how on earth are you going to be a missionary?" For the missions-minded North American evangelical, it's a legitimate question. But the question is not what is troubling. What is more disturbing is the common response, "Oh, I'm going as a teacher to get into the country so that I can do my *real job* of evangelism."

In this chapter, we will address why this undercover agent approach to missions lacks integrity and may actually hinder the teacher's effectiveness and authenticity. We also raise concerns regarding Christians' motives and purposes for teaching overseas. Finally, we challenge sincere and earnest Christians to reconsider this schizophrenic approach to overseas ministry and help them develop a sound and authentic vision for serving Christ in a distant classroom.

THE UNDERCOVER CHRISTIAN TEACHER

Teaching overseas is not merely a means to an end. Passionate followers of Christ should have no separation between the sacred and secular. For those of us who are in Christ Jesus, all that we do, say and are must come under his lordship. Therefore teaching in a distant classroom should not be just an excuse to gain access to a restricted country.

In a missions periodical on tentmaking, Peter Anderson (2001) wrote, "Could it not be argued that those who have a hidden religious agenda, while serving as professionals in a given field of expertise, are being dishonest? Are not honesty and integrity an essential part of our Christian life and witness? I believe they are" (p. 23). Anderson is right. This undercover Christian perspective can lack integrity and professional excellence. Once you view teaching as only an excuse, then you are not likely to teach well, nor model what is good. You are being disingenuous because you are in that nation teaching under false pretenses. This does not honor Christ.

Tentmaking is a term found in Acts 18 describing the work of the apostle Paul, Priscilla and Aquila as they used their skill and trade to be self-supporting in order to have an impact for Christ in foreign lands.

C. S. Lewis (1995), referring to the importance of honesty and integrity in teaching for Christian professors, wrote, "[A] Christian should not take money for supplying one thing (culture) [or we might say teaching] and use the opportunity thus gained to supply a quite different thing (homiletics and apologetics) [or we might say preaching]. That is stealing" (p. 221). The justification that one is simply volunteering at the university or institution still does not validate the undercover practice and attitude. Believers who volunteer their services to teach overseas should not take advantage of the opportunity to fulfill some hidden agenda. It is wrong. We are not to use the classroom lectern as a pulpit. Anderson (2001) explains:

> Those who go overseas to serve in their profession should see their job as the legitimate vehicle for their life and service and not just as the excuse for it. . . . They should be committed to their profession and through it demonstrate their commitment to Christ. (p. 24)

Commitment to your profession, whether at home or abroad, means seeing your vocation as an actual calling. Os Guinness (1998) warns Christians who attempt tentmaking without a sense of calling that

> such "tentmaking" at worst is work that *frustrates* us because it takes time we wish to spend on things [we consider] more central [such as Bible studies and personal evangelism]. By contrast, whatever is the heart of our calling is work that *fulfills* us because it employs our deepest gifts. (p. 52)

Teaching should flow out of a Christian's sense of calling. It should not be merely moonlighting. For the Christian educator, teaching in another land must be at the heart of her calling; it must be her *real job.*

Unfortunately in some cases, when Christians teach in another culture under false pretenses, they have actually discredited their witness. *The Economist* published a special report on Americans teaching English overseas:

> At the beginning of summer, hundreds of western missionaries . . . flock to Kazakhstan to teach English at local universities for a few weeks without pay. Many universities, hard up and unable to meet the huge demand for English, gladly accept. While it is certainly convenient, it is also controversial. Although missionaries are tolerated, local authorities suspect that the line between teaching and proselytizing is not always observed. A few years ago . . . Baptists offered "Bible aerobics" at an Almaty

university. Whatever this was, it wasn't teaching English. (Faith, 2001, p. 37.)

An authentic Christian witness is impossible when teaching is only a pretext for being in a foreign country. Such Christian educators are diluting their impact for Christ on students, colleagues and culture. This approach to teaching limits the concept of ministry to presenting the gospel, leading individuals in the right prayer, handing them Bibles and moving on to the next seeker. As a result all other work and activities, such as teaching, become less important.

Christian educators are called to be just that—Christian teachers, instructors or professors who strive to impact their students' lives with truth, integrity and honesty. Undercover Christian teachers may have some impact, but it is limited and their impact is in spite of their motives, not as a result of them.

CHECK YOUR MOTIVES

Motives are the driving force behind our goals, objectives and even our behavior. Before any Christian decides to resign his job, pack up his belongings and head overseas to teach, he must critically and honestly examine his motivation for going. This is a vital step in getting ready to teach in a distant classroom.

Jon Dybdahl (Baumgartner et al., 2002) in *Passport to Mission*, provides examples of various motives that prompt both Christians and non-Christians to move abroad. He argues that everyone has a mixture of both religious and nonreligious motives for overseas ministry. Although none of these motives are necessarily bad, Christian teachers need to examine and test their motives for wanting to teach overseas. Table 1 lists various reasons individuals choose to serve overseas.

At first the idea of crosscultural living may seem romantic and exciting. Certainly missions in the twenty-first century is not your grandfather's idea of missions. When pioneer missionaries in the nineteenth century set off to work among tribes in Africa, they packed their belongings in a coffin knowing that they would never set eyes

Table 1. Motives for Teaching Overseas. (Adapted from Jon L. Dybdahl, "So Why Not?" pp. 32-36 in Baumgartner et al., 2002.)

Nonreligious Motives for Overseas Teaching	Christian Motives for Overseas Teaching
Desire to travel and see the world	Called by God and prepared throughout life with gifts and experiences
Need a new career challenge or adventure	Have a heart for the people and truly desire for them to hear the gospel
Need a break from school or work	Love for Christ (2 Cor 5:14)
Consider overseas teaching as "selfless" work and others will think I am a good person (hero)	Scriptural incentive (Mt 9:37-38): "the harvest is plentiful but the workers are few"
Developing an international résumé	The Great Commission (Mt 28:18-20)
Curiosity or desire to experience other cultures and learn a new language	To be used to expose, persuade and lead others to Christ (Rom 1:18-20)
Career or job considerations	Have a true love and heart for the lost
Pressure from a parent, friend or spouse	"Come, follow me, and I will send you out to fish for people" (Mt 4:18-20)
Recruited by an organization and by default (not knowing anything better to do) decided to give it a try	I am going with an organization that enables me to use my God-given gifts
Escape from "the world" and isolate myself in a community not my own	The gospel of the kingdom will be preached to the whole world (Mt 24:14)

on family or homeland again. For the majority of these early missionaries, going to a distant land was not about adventure or excitement;
it was about duty—passionate, dedicated, sacrificial duty. But today a
modern missionary can arrive overseas in less than nine hours, grab
a Starbucks coffee before leaving the capital city, and begin a new life
right at home among towns and villages with McDonald's, Pizza Hut
and Hollywood movies. The Internet, air travel, satellite television,

---

Frank P., Ph.D., Physics, Cork, Ireland

My wife and I were always open to overseas missions. We struggled
with what I could do with a Ph.D. in physics. As I investigated missions
organizations, I also started applying for university jobs. That's when
God brought the two wonderfully together for me—an opportunity to
represent Christ at a secular university overseas while teaching the
subject I love.

Life was good for us in California. I had a big, beautiful house and
a good job. Our five children were thriving in their schools. My wife and
I were involved in various Christian ministries and outreach in our
community. Yet I couldn't shake the advice of a veteran missionary: "If
there are others nearby who can do your ministry, then go where there
isn't anyone else." That was the beginning. As we prayed together as
a family about where to go, we kept thinking the Middle East or China.
But God brought Ireland out of nowhere with a job posting that looked
like it had been lifted off my CV. I applied and got it.

We were very happy to go, but being in Ireland is hard. There are
huge cultural differences that have been fairly traumatic for our children at times. There is also a spiritual darkness here. It is a post-
Christian culture, and many of my students and fellow faculty members have a "been-there-done-that-bought-the-T-shirt" attitude toward
anything Christian.

Near the end of my first semester, I was encouraged by the physics
department to accept a leadership position at the research institute

global cell phones, Skype—all these things make going overseas seem much less permanent.

The good thing about globalization is that it has made missions easier. The bad thing about globalization is that it has made missions easier. It's good because more and more evangelicals are obeying Christ's command to go. More unreached people groups are hearing the good news of Jesus Christ, the Redeemer. Globalization has made

---

loosely affiliated with my university. To the astonishment of everyone, the research I was asked to supervise was actually based on my Ph.D. thesis work! They were so excited to learn I was the author of many of the initial research papers. I think they must be the only group in the world to have read my work, and God brought me right to them. This recognition brought instant respect and credibility.

Can you imagine the impact this has on my colleagues daily to think that a scientist they respect is a follower of Christ? Perhaps they think it is just some kind of fluke, but they *do* think about it.

During my second year at the department, I was asked to work on an application for a large research grant. This took weeks. This grant would give us the finances needed to do some great research and put our program on the map. After long months of work and waiting we got word: We received the grant! The whole thing was a big deal to my department and to my university. Thank God for his favor in these matters. It is all a part of earning the right to be heard here.

God has called us here and shown his faithfulness to us through relationships with neighbors, a good house to rent, conversations with students and fellow faculty. But spreading the gospel in Ireland is hard. We pray, we ask, we expect and most importantly we rest because he who has called us is faithful and he will do it. What we have to do is remain open, prayerful and sensitive to opportunities he arranges for us. Someone else could have filled the physics position, but I'm grateful that God allowed us to be here. The work is hard, slow and sometimes discouraging, but truly worth it.

missions more feasible and the Great Commission a truly attainable goal and task. However, with this great convenience comes a drawback. A majority of individuals who decide to go overseas as missionaries do not fully grasp the cost and the sacrifice of living incarnationally among those whom they serve. Globalization has made missions too easy and simplistic.

In order to be effective as a true witness for Christ in the distant classroom, a teacher's purposes for going must be Christ-centered as well as Christ-honoring. Globalization or not, challenges and difficulties still occur in a crosscultural context. Will your motives hold up when dealing with the demanding challenges that expatriate teachers face? That's when Christ's calling and infusion of strength are of utmost significance. During difficult times of misunderstandings, confusion and even perceived danger, you must know without a doubt Christ has called you to that place.

Teri works with the International Institute for Christian Studies (IICS) as part of a screening team for individuals and couples who want to teach overseas as a Christian mission. At the start of every interview she always asks, "What sense of calling, word from God or Scripture verse will you cling to when the worst imaginable thing happens to you far from home and family?" She asks because the desire for adventure, the need for employment or living by default are not strong enough to sustain an individual when faced with heartbreaking crises in a distant land. God's calling, the Spirit's impelling or a solid conviction of the Great Commission is absolutely essential for every Christian who wants to work or teach overseas.

Homesickness, frustrations with government and university bureaucracy, harsh living conditions, cultures that believe lying is a moral attribute—all of these can knock the adventure and excitement right out of the Christian worker. When the dust settles all that remains are motives that center on Christ and his calling. Only these can be an anchor in the stormy seas of crosscultural work. Motivation such as prestige, adventure and employment are not enough to hold anyone to his or her post when the going gets tough. Consider

---

Danny M., Ph.D., New Testament, Jos, Nigeria

I received a phone call this morning at 6:45 from John L. informing me that he and Char had been robbed about 2:30 a.m. by armed robbers. Apparently two men forced off the security bars in the front part of the house after confronting the security guards and taking away their cell phones. The robbers climbed through the window and were in John and Char's bedroom shining a light in their eyes before they were even aware of a problem. They demanded American money. They got $450 plus another 20,000 Naira (about $135). They took all three of their laptops.

Thankfully, John and Char weren't touched during the robbery. John estimated that the robbers were only in the house about four or five minutes. They seemed to be professionals, knowing where to find things. They had what appeared to be a sawed-off shotgun, which they stuck in John's face. They fired the gun as they left the house. The college security guards don't carry any weapons, so this would have been a warning for them not to follow.

This is obviously traumatic for John and Char. It is an unfortunate reality that God's work often goes forward through difficult and painful circumstances. John and Char have joined the ranks of other IICS staff at this university who have paid a price for their selfless service to the students and future leaders of Nigeria. We're praying that God will comfort and heal them and help replace those things that were lost. Though this event has robbed them of their possessions, we pray that it will not rob them of the joy they have experienced in serving the people here in Nigeria.

---

the attrition rate of global companies and programs: Xerox has a 63 percent attrition rate (Wederspahn, 2002). The Peace Corps' attrition rate, 30 percent overall (Tarnoff, 2002), is as high as *50 percent* in countries such as Nepal (Hetrick, 1999). About 30 to 60 percent of all Peace Corps workers go home before their contracts are completed.

AM I CALLED TO CROSSCULTURAL TEACHING?

What does it mean to be called to a ministry? Guinness (1998) defines calling in this way:

> Calling is the truth that God calls us to himself so decisively that everything we are, everything we do, and everything we have is invested with a special devotion and dynamism lived out as a response to his summons and service. (p. 4)

There is little doubt that God calls all of us to service. But perhaps not all of us are called to minister crossculturally. So when does God call people to long-term, foreign missionary service? How do you know if you have an overseas missions call?

Some Christians say, "If you don't hear 'no,' then go." Scripture does compel us to go. Missions exists because Jesus commanded us to go: "Go into all the world and proclaim the good news to the whole creation" (Mk 16:15 NRSV). But missions isn't about *me* and about making *me* feel good. It is not about being fulfilled, finding a "purpose" or going on some great adventure.

Simply, *missions is about obedience.* Missions is about bringing glory to God and Jesus Christ. It's about sharing truth and hope with those who are in desperate need. It's about exalting God's name among the nations. It is privileged participation in what God is doing around the world. The moment missions stops being about God and Jesus Christ and starts being about me, then disingenuous motives come into play and problems develop.

Mike has had many opportunities to counsel and listen to young adults. Some of his Christian students believe they are called to the foreign mission field. But when these students say that teaching in a far country would help them develop their résumés, he knows there's a problem. Alarms also go off when young college graduates feel like overseas ministry is an obligation—something they should and must do. He always challenges his students to be honest with themselves and ask, "Why am I really going abroad to teach?" Here are a few questions that might help you determine the "why" of your going to a distant land.

QUESTIONS ABOUT MOTIVES

1. Why am I going overseas?

2. What do I hope to accomplish while I am there?

3. Have I said to myself, "If I don't like it there, I can always come home"?

4. Would I still be willing to go if I knew in advance that I would lose my life by going? Am I willing to give my life for this purpose?

5. How does my going affect what others think of me? How does their opinion of me affect my going?

6. If going to teach in a particular country made me somehow unemployable later in my life, would I still be willing to go?

QUESTIONS ABOUT TEACHING

1. Am I equipped to teach? If not, then what am I doing to become equipped?

2. Have others confirmed to me that I am a good teacher?

3. Have I taught before? If so, do I like teaching?

4. If I am not qualified to teach in my home country, then how qualified am I to teach in an overseas setting?

5. Has anyone to whom I am spiritually accountable (a pastor, a small-group leader or a Christian friend) confirmed to me that teaching abroad is a good fit for me?

QUESTIONS ABOUT GETTING THERE

1. What type of missions organization am I considering?

2. Does my chosen organization have high standards and requirements?

3. Are they good stewards of their finances? What do they require of me financially?

4. Do they provide adequate crosscultural training and preparation?

5. What kind of support, both moral and spiritual, do they offer me while overseas?

6. Is the organization focused on serving a particular people group with a clear vision for that group? (Talk with others who have been involved with this organization and do your homework to determine if this is a group for you.)

7. Do I have a strong prayer support base at home? (You must have a strong and faithful prayer support base at home that will intercede for specific prayer requests as well as for effectiveness in your work and calling.)

8. Do I have accountability in place in the setting where I will be serving? Is there a church, a group of Christians or another believer with whom I can worship and fellowship?

God calls us to give him our very best. When Christians accept teaching assignments abroad they must be committed to high standards, to being professionally prepared and truly committed to teaching well. Living a life of integrity and working with excellence are the crucial foundations of effectiveness in overseas ministry. If students and colleagues don't respect your teaching, or feel you lack professionalism, then they surely won't be interested in attending a Bible study in your home or hearing what you have to say about Christianity.

Frank Hawes and Daniel Kealey (cited in Elmer, 2000) did a study on crosscultural living and found these two basic generalizations to be true:

• Most people of the world do not separate the person from his/her work.

• If the host national values the work of the expatriate, then he/she will like the person as well.

I (Teri) was part of a team invited by UNESCO to train university faculty in Kabul, Afghanistan. The Ministry of Higher Education made it clear they wanted the laws of the land obeyed: no evangelism, no proselytizing, no hidden agendas. The team went to Kabul know-ing we might not have an opportunity to share our faith. We went anyway because workshops, seminars and interaction with faculty were all ministry, even if Jesus' name wasn't mentioned.

While I was conducting a workshop on higher education, a man stood up and said, "Dr. Teri, do you believe in Muhammad?" I paused and tried to think of a win-win response. "Of course. He is a histori-cal figure with . . ."

The man interrupted, "No! I mean, do you believe he is the prophet of Allah?" I was stuck. Participants' heads went down; no one looked around. It felt as if it was just the two of us in the room.

"I defend your right to believe that," I responded and tried to steer the conversation toward democracy and freedom of speech. But the man was persistent. "Do you follow Muhammad or Jesus?" he asked.

I hesitated and then answered, "Jesus." He shouted back, "Mu-hammad is greater than Jesus!" I looked at him. He shouted, "Say it! Say that Muhammad is greater than Jesus!" I couldn't and prayed si-lently for direction.

Knowing Afghanis' respect for family, I replied, "If I said those words it would break my grandmother's heart. Do you want me to disgrace my grandmother and break her heart?"

The man was surprised by this response and stumbled a bit. Then an elderly, well-respected professor raised his hand. "Dr. Teri, may I say something?" Everyone in the room sighed relief. "Muhammad taught us that Jesus was a great and wonderful teacher. We know that Dr. Teri is a follower of his because she too is a great and wonderful teacher. To be quite frank, even our own prophet Muhammad would not ask Dr. Teri to say such a thing. The Qur'an teaches that God will reveal himself to anyone who seeks him, whether that be in a mosque, a church or a temple." He paused and said, "May I write that verse on the board, Dr. Teri?"

I handed him the chalk. Just about then the bell rang and everyone headed for lunch—except four men who waited for the classroom to empty. Then they asked, "Dr. Teri, we have always wanted to learn more about Jesus. Can you help us? Do you have some literature or articles we can read that will help us to understand him and to learn more about him?" I did.

We don't have to bring Jesus into the classroom. He's already there. By praying and trusting God, walking in obedience and doing our work as unto him, the team in Afghanistan never had to break any rules, manipulate any hidden agendas or go against classroom protocol. And still God showed up.

Living a life of integrity means being authentic and genuine and doing all things well. It means giving your all in both preparation and task. Poor teaching hurts the Christian witness and the cause of Christ. We must take our teaching seriously and see our teaching as the true calling for our overseas service. When well-meaning friends and family ask us, "If you can't talk about Jesus in the classroom, how can you be effective for the kingdom?" we can wholeheartedly reply, "By doing my *real job* of teaching for his glory and in his name."

GOING DEEPER, GOING FURTHER

Questions to Consider

1. What are your motives for overseas teaching? Develop a list and sort them into religious and nonreligious motives. Which are your strongest motives?

2. Consider how God has led you to this point in your life. What has he done in your life to prepare you for this calling?

3. What personal characteristics do you have that will help you be successful living and teaching overseas?

4. What are your goals for living and teaching in a distant land?

Exercise/Activities

Examining Your Call (Lee, 1996):
Are you truly called to teach overseas? The following steps can help you determine this call:

Step 1: Begin with an open heart and open mind.

Step 2: Examine the Scriptures. The following look at some specific missionary calls:

Ephesians 3:1-13

Matthew 28:18-20

Exodus 3

Jeremiah 1

Jonah 1

Step 3: Be open and listen to the Holy Spirit.

Step 4: Read missionary biographies, country-specific information and any material that provides a global perspective (such as *Operation World*, Johnstone & Mandryke, 2001).

Step 5: Seek wise counsel.

Step 6: Talk with others who have overseas experience.

Step 7: Pray specifically for clarity and direction.

God's call must not be based solely on feelings, but a balance between counsel, facts, promptings and yes, open doors.

Suggested Readings and Helpful Websites

Articles

"The Academic Witness: Research and Scholarship As Unto the Lord," Jay Budziszewski, *The Real Issue*, September/October 2001

"Ministry, Profits and the Schizophrenic Tentmaker," Steve Rundle, *Evangelical Missions Quarterly* 36, no. 3 (2000): 292-300

"The Two Tasks," Charles Malik, *Journal of the Evangelical Theological Society* 23, no. 4, December 1980

Books

Avoiding the Tentmaker Trap, Dan Gibson

Working Your Way to the Nations: A Guide to Effective Tentmaking, Jonathan Lewis

Your Mind Matters: The Place of the Mind in the Christian Life, John
   Stott

Websites

http://www.adventistvolunteers.org/Forms/Passport.pdf

http://www.iics.com

http://www.godisatwork.org

http://www.tentmakernet.com

REFERENCE LIST

Anderson, P. (2001). Is tentmaking dishonest? *World Christian, 14,*
   23-24.

Baumgartner, E. W., Dybdahl, J. L., Gustin, P., & Moyer, B. C. (2002).
   Passport to mission (2nd ed.). Anderson University, Berrien Springs,
   MI: Institute of World Mission.

Elmer, D. (2000). Trust: A good start on crosscultural effectiveness.
   Trinity World Forum, 25(2), 1-4.

Faith in politics. (2001, August 25). *The Economist, 359,* 37.

Guinness, O. (1998). *The call: Finding and fulfilling the central purpose
   of your life.* Nashville: Word Publishing.

Hetrick, J. (1999). Wildlife, politics and policies. *Journal of Research
   and Creative Activity, 21*(3), 20-23.

Johnstone, P., & Mandryke, J. (2001). *Operation world.* Carlisle, UK:
   Paternoster.

Lee, D. T. W. (1996). Cross-cultural servants. In J. Lewis (Ed.), *Working your way to the nations: A guide to effective tentmaking* (pp. 27-
   40). Downers Grove, IL: InterVarsity Press.

Lewis, C. S. (1995). *Christian reflections.* Grand Rapids: Eerdmans.

Tarnoff, C. (2002, March 8). The Peace Corps: USA Freedom Corps
   initiative. *CRS Report for Congress.*

Wederspahn, G. M. (2002). Making the case for intercultural training. *International Human Resource Management Journal, 9*(2),
   309-31.

2

What Does My Worldview Have to Do with Teaching?

The key premise of a Christian worldview is that all truth is God's truth. Abraham Kuyper, the great Dutch Reformed leader and former prime minister of Holland, said, "In the total expanse of human life there is not a single square inch of the entire universe of which the Christ, who alone is sovereign, does not declare, 'That is mine!'" (as cited in Vanden Berg, 1978, p. 255). In an attempt to live out a Christian worldview as educators overseas, we must realize that our teaching, and our academic disciplines, matter to Christ. We must explore what it means when Jesus says of each of our lives, "That is mine!" And more particularly as teachers, we must understand what it means when Jesus says of teaching, "That belongs to me!"

Whether teaching in Africa, Asia, Latin America or Europe, educators need to develop a sound understanding of how they see and interpret the world around them. How we view the world, knowingly and unknowingly, impacts the way we teach. All teaching is based on the teacher's worldview. This influences the teacher's philosophy of education, relationships with students, effectiveness as a teacher and even the details of lesson planning. By understanding a Christian worldview of teaching and learning, we come to terms with who we are and how, why and what we teach.

In this chapter we will look at the factors that shape our worldview and the role of worldview—how it answers the questions of our lives, how it influences the way we see and interpret everything around us, and how it shapes the teaching-learning process.

TEACHING IS MORE THAN
LESSON PLANS AND METHODS

"Good teaching cannot be reduced to technique; good teaching comes from the identity and integrity of the teacher" (Palmer, 1998, p. 10). Too often inexperienced or uninformed teachers reduce teaching to the practical or technical while unknowingly tossing aside the underpinnings of values and beliefs of teaching. As mere technicians, teachers become "efficient distributors of information who neglect the more critical aspects of culture and schooling" (Giroux & McLaren, 1996, p. 304).

The Christian educator who reduces teaching to simply distributing information fails to understand the importance of teaching Christianly. By being mere technicians, we fail to serve students as "unto Christ." This impedes building genuine relationships with students and teaching them effectively. Reducing teaching to the simple transmission of knowledge, be it business, English or engineering, fails to demonstrate the holistic and comprehensive nature of Christ's lordship that seeks to glorify God in all of life and learning. This problem occurs because the teaching process is oversimplified and the most important questions about teaching and education are rendered insignificant.

Technicians are more concerned with the mastering and refining of information than they are with challenging and influencing students and in turn "transforming many of the basic cultural institutions and belief systems" (Purpel, 1989, p. 3). As Christian educators in overseas classrooms, part of our calling as followers of Christ is to be agents of transformation in culture and society. Our motivation for teaching in a distant land is to make a difference. If we fall into the trap of reducing our teaching to technical output, then we miss our main objective. Grabbing a set of prepackaged curriculum for teaching English, throwing it in a suitcase and heading overseas without reflection on what it means to teach Christianly reduces the beauty and purpose of education to simply the technical. It reduces us to mere technicians.

THE INNER TERRAIN

The teacher's identity and integrity grow out of what Palmer (1998) terms "the inner terrain" (p. 5). Although seldom addressed in lecture halls, seminars or crosscultural training programs, the "inner terrain" encompasses teachers' experiences as children and adults, our likes and dislikes, and the vast number of events that make up who we are—including our beliefs, values and ultimate concerns. It is about our biases, our faith, our sense of morality and how we see ourselves. By considering our inner terrain, we are better able to understand who we are as human beings and teachers.

Teaching is about how we view the world and what the world should look like. Our inner terrain shows up in the way we respond to the class clown or handle students cheating. The inner terrain is revealed in our lesson plans and class objectives. It can be seen in our desire to push an agenda rather than to focus on our students' needs. It manifests itself even if we are unaware of it. Christian teaching is about filtering all things through a Christian worldview. Our inner terrain should reflect a biblically informed, Christ-centered perspective.

Because teaching is about who we are and not just what

Pedagogy: **the art and science of educating students. The term is often used as a synonym for teaching. Pedagogy is the strategies, techniques and approaches that teachers can use to facilitate learning.**

we teach, it requires an honest discernment of "what is integral to my selfhood: what fits and what does not" (Palmer, 1998, p. 13). We must invite the Holy Spirit into our lives and ask for his help in self-discovery, questioning, reflection and eventually awareness and change. This process starts by simply asking questions. If in fact I teach *who* I am, then I must ask, "Who am I?" If teachers truly teach from our beliefs, then we must ask, "What do I believe?" If our biases shape our pedagogy, then we must identify those biases and discern if they are in line with what is honoring to Christ. We must deliberately look at our motives, teaching style, methods and teacher-student relationships and ask, "Why am I doing it this way?"

Not surprisingly, all teachers bring their "life luggage" to the blackboard. This has a strong impact on our pedagogy and directly influences students—either for good or for ill. Life luggage with prejudices, misconceptions and stereotypes can be harmful in the classroom. If they remain unchecked, they not only obstruct the learning process but they communicate powerful messages and damaging principles to our students.

On the other hand, a Christian educator's life luggage can be an asset if properly understood and addressed. If we believe that Christ adds value to a classroom and that God's perspective is truth, then bringing our life luggage into the classroom isn't all bad. But there need to be safeguards. A Christian worldview doesn't mean we have the right to force our belief system on others, such as artificially forcing opportunities for personal evangelism in the classroom. We must guard against manipulating students into Bible-topic conversations that are not related to the course or lesson. Self-analysis and reflection helps the believer learn to honor Christ in her teaching skills, academic discipline and student-teacher relationships so that students are benefited and true learning takes place. Self-analysis is about letting go of cultural assumptions regarding learning and teaching and being open to new and different ways of approaching the classroom.

TEACHERS' INNER TERRAIN
DISCOVERING OUR HIDDEN WORLDVIEWS

Teaching is a complicated task saturated with personal values and beliefs that are communicated both explicitly and implicitly in the classroom. Since teaching requires some form of evaluation and interpretation, teachers constantly make choices and decisions based on their own views. As a result, the teaching process is never value-free or neutral. Beneath every classroom practice is a teacher's worldview that is composed of what he or she believes to be true, to be valuable, what is important, what is right and wrong, and what is real.

For instance, a college-level Composition I instructor is frustrated by students' inability to spell. She has never had a problem with spelling and won spelling contests in junior high. Her father wasn't very affirming to her as a child, but he always praised her gift for spelling. Spelling is personally significant to her, and that fact reveals itself in her professional life in two ways: through her strict rules about spelling (two misspelled words in an assignment is an "F") and in her visible overreaction and frustration toward students who continually misspell words.

Is spelling essential in the writing process? Yes. Is she too focused on it? Perhaps. But this excessive focus comes from her inner terrain and is a result of her personal experiences with spelling. It is part of her life luggage—something she probably is not even aware of—yet it impacts students' learning. It negatively affects their thoughts and feelings about Composition I. Most significantly, it distorts their perception of her as a teacher.

Christian educators must be reflective. We need self-analysis and critical evaluation to prevent our life luggage from hindering teaching that truly represents a Christian worldview. This requires Christian teachers to develop a critical eye that not only raises important questions about educational issues, but about their own teaching and approaches to the classroom.

COMPONENTS OF A WORLDVIEW

To start, let's look at the components of a worldview. James Sire (2004) developed a comprehensive and insightful definition of a worldview:

> A commitment, a fundamental orientation of the heart, that can be expressed as a story or in a set of presuppositions (assumptions that may be true, partially true or entirely false) which we hold (consciously or subconsciously, consistently or inconsistently) about the basic constitution of reality, and that provides the foundation on which we live and move and have our being. (p. 122)

This definition introduces several key issues that are relevant for teaching abroad. Sire (2004) points out that a worldview contains our beliefs about reality that make up the most inner core of who we are. Some of these beliefs are based on our culture or upbringing. These commitments differ from person to person. Our beliefs about reality are influenced by such factors as family dynamics, faith communities, personal life-altering events and, most importantly, culture.

For most people, these commitments are developed subconsciously. We are usually unaware of how they manifest themselves in our actions or motives. Worldviews often collide when people from differing cultures get together. Here's an illustration:

> Troy and Jane hosted a Chinese couple to come live with them while the couple attended graduate school in the U.S. Troy and Jane were excited to have this couple from China. They were eager to be good hosts to their guests. Troy and Jane owned a dog named Snoodie. Snoodie slept with them, ate near the kitchen table and occasionally had accidents in the house when they were away too long during the day.
>
> Lee and Chang were raised in Northeast China where some of the population thought of dog meat as a delicacy. Their city was home to several famous dog-meat restaurants. Due to communist regulations and overcrowding in the city, China's gov-

ernment did not allow citizens to keep dogs as pets. In fact, Lee and Chang believed dogs to be dirty, because they had only seen outdoor working dogs from farms or the occasional unpleasant guard dog. Lee and Chang were frightened of dogs and never experienced the luxury of having a pet.

When Lee and Chang moved in with Troy and Jane, they were shocked to see what they considered a filthy animal living in the house. They were utterly confused by the animal's eating near the kitchen table. They were disgusted by the idea that the dog slept with her masters. The occasional accident on the rug was appalling to them.

Soon after they arrived, Lee and Chang decided they had to find another place to live. Because Chinese tradition mandates nonconfrontation, they moved without any clear explanation why. Troy and Jane, having no previous experience with Chinese culture, immediately concluded that Chinese people are very strange and rather rude. Lee and Chang concluded that Americans love their animals more than people.

Troy and Jane and Lee and Chang all had worldviews that contained deeply held beliefs about the basis of reality. These were hidden in their inner terrain. Cultural conflicts occurred because the two couples were operating from two different worldviews so deeply ingrained that they could not recognize the validity or even the existence of the other. This often happens in the overseas classroom.

These basic beliefs or commitments are not always consistent. Individuals can lack an awareness of the contradiction between what a stated worldview is and their actual behavior. We see an example of this in the lives of those who drafted the U.S. Declaration of Independence. They wrote "that all men are created equal, that they are endowed by their Creator with certain unalienable rights . . . the right to life, liberty and the pursuit of happiness." Yet except for Benjamin Franklin and John Adams, each of these men was a slaveholder. There was a clear contradiction between their stated worldview and their behavior.

Worldviews are usually unconscious. As Sire (2004) states, "We are thinking with it, not about it" (p. 130). Sire points out that "our worldview is not precisely what we may state it to be. It is what is actualized in our behavior. We live our worldview or it isn't our worldview" (p. 133).

Individuals often uncritically take their worldviews for granted as the "normal" way of seeing things, like Troy and Jane who believed that having a dog in the house is acceptable. They didn't realize that to their guests their love for their dog seemed more important than Lee and Chang's comfort. Most of us seldom consciously reflect upon the components of our worldviews, but rather we allow our assumptions and life commitments to influence our thinking and behavior. We can live comfortably with this as long as we don't cross borders. But when we enter a foreign culture, our assumptions about life are challenged. If we don't understand worldview differences, we can come across as arrogant and inflexible and cause great isolation between us and the culture we are called to serve.

WORLDVIEW QUESTIONS

Thinking Christianly about teaching requires that we develop a frame of reference or a worldview that is based on Christian presuppositions. What are those assumptions, and where does a Christian worldview begin? Sire (2004) raises fundamental questions that everyone answers whether by design or default. They are as follows:

1 What is the prime reality—the really real?

2. What is the nature of external reality, that is, the world around us?

3. What is a human being?

4. What happens to persons at death?

5. Why is it possible to know anything at all?

6. How do we know what is right and wrong?

7. What is the meaning of human history? (p. 20)

These questions are the starting point of a worldview. An individual's responses to these questions serve as the basis of her worldview (her perceptions of events and experiences). Keep in mind that a worldview never belongs to just one individual but is shared among a culture (Walsh & Middleton, 1984). So when interacting in our home culture, these assumptions are usually "unquestioned by each of us, rarely if ever mentioned by our friends, and brought to mind only when we are challenged by a foreigner from another ideological universe" (Sire, 2004, p. 20).

When living crossculturally, the expatriate is confronted with diverse ways of seeing the world. Simple things such as table manners, social discourse and even eye contact can move from innate natural responses to cultural faux pas. This can shake the expatriate to his very core, challenging his perceptions of right and wrong and dos and don'ts. When confronted with the host culture's different ways of thinking, individuals overseas are often forced to examine and explain their own positions in ways they may have never done before. They must examine not only the foundation of their worldview, but they must be able to articulate it and to explain the reasoning and validity behind it. Because of this, self-reflection and analysis is not only necessary for the classroom, but for all of life. Part of forming a well-developed Christian worldview of life and vocation is evaluating what in my life luggage is of God and what is simply of my culture.

WORLDVIEWS GUIDE OUR LIVES

Worldviews are not simply a vision *of* life, but rather a vision *for* life (Walsh & Middleton, 1984). The difference is significant. Having a vision *of* life states what we think *ought* to be, while a vision *for* life determines how we live. A vision for life "governs both the unconscious actions we engage in and the actions we ponder before acting" (Sire, 2004, p. 99). Thus worldviews are perceptual frameworks based on an elaborate set of beliefs that guide behavior and thoughts. They are interwoven into the fabric of personal and professional lives whether deliberately or by default. They are the automatic settings of our daily lives by which we make all our decisions. Therefore it is vital to know what we believe and why we believe it. Through reflection and self-analysis, we must deliberately evaluate our worldviews and remove what is incorrect and harmful while adding what is true and edifying. Our worldviews then move from living by default to living decisively, to truly reflect who we are and what we believe.

Developing consistency in what we believe and how we act is absolutely essential for those living and teaching overseas. Inconsistencies between beliefs and behavior can result from a lack of awareness or an inability to gain access to our worldview presuppositions. The average secular American may survive and thrive with such inconsistencies, but for Christians living and teaching overseas it simply is not acceptable. Students quickly discover the contradictions and can actually receive a very different message than we intended to convey. When a Christian educator demands that her students show respect by turning in their homework on time, she must demonstrate consistency, showing the students this same respect by returning their homework in a fair and timely manner. In teaching, our behavior and beliefs have a strong impact on our students. Inconsistencies between what we say and what we do are interpreted as a lack of sincerity.

WHAT INFLUENCES AND SHAPES OUR WORLDVIEW?

Many factors and influences shape how North Americans see the world. Walsh and Middleton (1984) list several factors that influence one's worldview, including education, family, politics, legal institutions, environmental concerns, healthcare, religious institutions and the arts. Others with tremendous power include race, social class, the media and gender. The following discussion focuses on what we consider the five most significant factors that play a role in shaping one's worldview and eventually a teacher's pedagogy.

First, worldviews are learned through socialization and social interaction. They are constantly being reinforced by culture and society throughout a lifetime. When individuals belong to a specific socioeconomic or ethnic group, they derive some aspects of their sense of identity from that particular group. For instance, an integral part of Americans' worldviews is the belief that individual freedom is central to life. Most Americans view the world based upon the concept of democracy. They develop a sense of identity by making comparisons with other groups and cultures: democratic societies are our allies; nondemocratic societies are our enemies.

In addition, individuals possess social and personal histories that saturate their worldviews. Social histories reflect how the social and economic structures shape individuals' lives and the manner in which they view the world. For example, Mike's own social history of growing up in a poor working-class family near Wilkes-Barre, Pennsylvania, has influenced how he views and treats the disadvantaged both in and out of the classroom. This social history influenced his responses while teaching in China:

> During my stay in China, I was frustrated by the caste or hierarchical system that existed in this so-called egalitarian society. The dislike and discrimination of the underprivileged in China was very blatant and difficult for me to accept. Many Chinese were taken aback that a well-educated American professor would be willing to talk to the young man who delivered bottled water, the woman who sold fruit, the workers on the street and the woman who collected trash. They were shocked, and some were offended, when our family bought these individuals Christmas gifts. I wanted to reach out to these people because of how I was treated as a kid. My worldview of how the underclass should be treated was clearly influenced by my own social history of living in poverty, my recollection of feelings of inferiority, and my remembrance of the experiences and effects of being poor in a rich country. The intellectuals in China found my behavior disturbing.

The complexities of social histories are not limited to social class but also include categories of gender, race, age and ethnicity. These categories are intertwined. There is no doubt that a poor African

American woman sees and experiences the world much differently than a wealthy British white male. Chinese students educated in a communist school system view the world differently than a student from an affluent private boarding school in Switzerland.

Personal history, although tangled with social and economic experiences, differs in that it is derived from personal characteristics, individual relationships and familial experiences. Personality traits such as indecisiveness, the need to control or dominate, achievement orientation or perfectionism can all play a role in how we view the world and relate to people. Our personal history covers an unlimited range of areas that includes travel, interaction with others, relationships, events, good and bad experiences, upbringing and faith communities. All these and more make up the history of our lives.

Second, a worldview is shared among a culture. Culture and ideology are deeply ingrained in people's lives and play a significant role in shaping worldviews. Through our travels and educational experiences abroad, we (the authors) have realized that the American worldview differs significantly from that of other nations, even from those of our Canadian cousins. Viewing the world from a capitalistic, democratic and individualistic perspective, and as citizens of one of the most powerful nations, certainly colors the manner in which we understand important issues and daily activities. One of Mike's students told a humorous story that shows how culture shapes the way people view the world and how those views differ:

> A teacher has four students in her classroom. One student is from Western Europe, one from Africa, one from China and one is from the United States. She challenges the class with an assignment. They are to write their opinions about food shortages in another country.
>
> As they struggle with the assignment, each student has a question for the teacher. The student from Europe asks, "What is a shortage?" The African student inquires about the meaning of the word "food." The Chinese student is puzzled because he

needs the teacher to explain what an opinion is. The American needs to know, "What is another country?"

Make no mistake—people from every culture struggle in crosscultural settings. Americans' worldviews are marinated in several dominant ideologies that shape Americans' ways of seeing things. The ideology of merit, that "anyone can be anything they want to be if they work hard enough," has dominated American thinking for decades. Oakes and Lipton (1999) argue that this ideology has been a source of national pride because Americans believe they have developed a culture "in which individual ability and determination, rather than wealth or personal connections, hold the key to success and upward mobility" (pp. 15-16). This thinking allows people with privilege "to believe that their own wealth and happiness stand on a moral platform of merit" (p. 18). Basing individual success solely on merit excludes any discussion about the role economics, social class, personal crises or even catastrophe can play on an individual's motivations, aspirations, beliefs, performance and overall view of life.

Concurrently, Americans are strongly influenced by what has been called the "busyness philosophy." As a culture, Americans lead overstuffed lives filled with cell phones, laptops, activities, work and material consumption. Many individuals (Christians too) base their worth on their performance or activities. We are a culture of doers. We believe what we do defines who and what we are.

This addictive busyness is present in every aspect of American culture and substitutes activity for relationships. This busyness ideology clearly shapes how Americans view the world. Think about the idiom "You snooze, you lose." When Americans learn that the Chinese take a *wǔ shuì* or afternoon nap, many think that is a sign of laziness. Americans usually want to know if the Chinese work later into the day to make up missed work hours. Americans view the *wǔ shuì* as inefficient and think so much more could be accomplished if this time was better spent—working. This ideology and others shape the way we see the world, students and learning.

Third, institutions play a significant role in the construction of an individual's worldview. In North America, Hollywood and the media, family, church, corporations, and governmental institutions influence people's understanding of themselves and the world. The U.S. is renowned for films that portray women as unrealistically beautiful and thin. These influence young women's self-image and can result in eating disorders that some women battle all their lives. Individuals' worldviews are also shaped by governmental institutions that promote out-of-balance nationalism, as in Germany under Hitler. All countries and cultures have worldview influencers.

Fourth, education shapes the way individuals see the world. Education, through the lives and practices of teachers, impacts our thinking, our interaction with others, and the way we view ourselves and the world. Teachers impact students' lives and their worldviews. Education changes the way people think and in turn changes, challenges or reinforces the worldviews that guide their lives.

This is clearly seen in the life of Osama bin Laden, who has said that his worldview was fundamentally changed by one university professor. Bin Laden, described by classmates as shy and nonreligious, was an engineering major in Saudi Arabia when he took a class from a Palestinian-born Islamic radical. This one professor, according to bin Laden, inspired his religious fervor and set him on the course of extreme Islamic fundamentalism. Apparently this professor's commitment to the Qur'an, simple lifestyle and passion for Islam transformed the young bin Laden, forever changing his life and eventually our world. Education is a transmitter of worldviews—for better or worse.

Finally, worldviews are based on faith or some type of religious belief system. Even in atheistic cultures, people operate from a set of assumptions—articles of faith that form their particular worldview. For the life of the Christian, our faith provides us with meaning and direction in life. It shapes our view of the world, our sense of morality, and guides our decisions and behavior—or at least it should. As Christians who are teachers, we have an excellent starting point in forming a Christian worldview of education found in Scripture and in Christian thought.

THE ROLE OF WORLDVIEW AND
BELIEFS IN TEACHING

Worldviews are essential for teachers to grasp because they shape the way teachers define and understand physical and social realities. They also foster schools of thought and are inevitably intertwined with knowledge that is taught or omitted from the classroom. When an instructor teaches from a particular worldview, whether intentionally or not, they select, omit and restructure knowledge and curriculum. Values are being transferred in the classroom not only through what we teach, but also through the way we teach. Therefore, a Christian worldview of education must understand that all educational practices convey values and ideas that shape our students.

C. S. Lewis (1944/1996) warned teachers in 1940s England not to create "men without chests." In other words, do not create students lacking in a value system and the ability to differentiate between right and wrong. Lewis's point was that even in the teaching of English, good values must be conveyed. "It is the doctrine of objective value, the belief that certain attitudes are really true and others really false, to the kind of thing the universe is and the kind of things we are" (p. 31). Lewis's Christian worldview enabled him to make a stand against the relativism presented in an English textbook. He eloquently explained that ideas have consequences and that teaching is a grave responsibility because teachers influence how students see the world. Lewis challenges educators to think about what they are teaching.

Nowhere is this principle better illustrated than in the Student Democracy Movement in the People's Republic of China in the 1980s. After Deng Xiao Ping's Open Door Policy in 1979, literally thousands of Christian English as a Foreign Language (EFL) teachers rushed to China. As a result, ideas and values were conveyed in EFL classrooms that were explicitly pro-Western and prodemocracy. In response, Deng, encouraged by top Party leaders, announced that English words could be learned using Chinese ideas. The Party believed, erroneously, that the much-needed English language could be taught without affecting communist ideals. Their slogan became "Teach Mao's thoughts when teaching the English language." However, the Western teachers of EFL continued to carry the contagious virus of democracy and freedom into the Chinese EFL classroom through simple conversational exercises and the learning of American folksongs. The final outcome was the Student Democracy Movement of 1989, which tragically ended with the Tiananmen massacre. Dovring (1997) explains,

> The young intellectuals' and workers' uprising under the banner of *democracy* and *equality* and under the eyes of the image of the American Statue of Liberty gave the ruling junta bloody proof of what may happen when the students are ordered to speak Chinese communism in foreign languages. The process backfired and foreign ideas and values took over under the cover of linguistics. (p. 16)

Dovring affirms Lewis's (1944/1996) idea that no teaching is value neutral. Something is being taught other than history, math or language; this is inevitable. Since neutrality or value-free teaching is impossible, teachers should understand the process by which values, beliefs and worldviews influence knowledge and teaching strategies in the classroom. Figure 1 illustrates some of the influences that shape worldviews and how a worldview is transformed into a teacher's pedagogy.

The teacher uses her worldview as a *vision for life* and develops a philosophy of education, either by default or design. The teacher's philosophy is then placed into the practical realm by integrating her teaching methods, curriculum and other educational practices in the classroom. Here methods, curriculum and teacher-student interactions intersect, and students have opportunities to learn beliefs, values and knowledge.

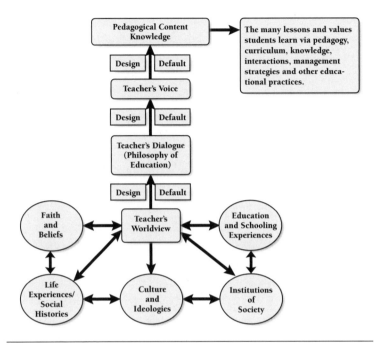

Figure 1. Worldview influences and teaching. (Adapted from Romanowski, 1998.)

THE CHRISTIAN MIND,
BIBLICAL WORLDVIEWS AND TEACHING

Harry Blamires (1963/2005) stated over forty years ago that

> there is no longer a Christian mind. . . . As a thinking being, the
> modern Christian has succumbed to secularization. He accepts
> religion—its morality, its worship, its spiritual culture; but he
> rejects the religious view of life, the view which sets all earthly
> issues within the context of the eternal, the view which relates
> all human problems—social, political, cultural—to the doctri-
> nal foundations of the Christian faith. (pp. 3-4)

Philosopher William Hasker (1992) argues that the integration of
faith is "a scholarly project whose goal is to ascertain and to develop
integral relationships which exist between the Christian faith and

human knowledge, particularly as expressed in the various academic disciplines" (p. 231). Christian educators must foster a keen interest in the integral relationships between faith and knowledge and develop a biblical worldview of their academic discipline. As Frank Gaebelein (1968) points out, the integration of their faith and learning includes themselves as the teacher as well as the subject matter, students, school and classroom.

First, Christian educators must blend the principles of a biblical worldview into their academic discipline regardless of what that discipline is. Physics, history, political science, the humanities, business and law all come under the lordship of Jesus Christ. If all truth is God's truth, then all disciplines are his.

For example, Christian professor Paul Gibson taught soil science and seed genetics at a university in Ukraine. Some missions organizations might think that Dr. Gibson's field of soil science isn't significant for the kingdom. But it was a critically important topic in that nation, which struggled with its agricultural development and need to feed its citizens. Gibson developed a soybean seed that is resistant to mold, and this influenced the way his students thought about Christianity. For many of them, he was the first intellectual they had ever met who professed faith in Christ. Emerging from a communist government, they believed the term "Christian academic" was an oxymoron. But no one could doubt the incredible contribution Gibson's mold-resistant seed made on crop production there. This development benefited his students, his university and the nation he was called to serve.

Some North American Christians might believe that church planting is the only significant work that can be done overseas. But Jesus Christ is revealed to nations not just through church planting, but in soil science—and other fields as well. Truly a revelation of Christ occurs when a Christian professor like Dr. Gibson uses his talents, gifts and abilities to honor God and to serve others in a university classroom.

Christ cares about our academic discipline. Our areas of expertise can bring Christ into the lives of our students and even into the very fiber of the nation. From a Christian worldview, teaching English, for example, is as important as teaching New Testament. Studies have shown that marginalized women living in extreme poverty in developing countries are empowered to rise above their economic and social status by learning English (Snow, 2000). By developing strong English-language skills, these women become employable because their skills are necessary for international commerce and trade. Once these women are employed and make a living wage, they and their children can emerge from poverty and gain respect in the community. They are empowered to end the vicious cycle of poverty and unemployment, and their children can get good educations, are fed and receive medical care. Surely this is God-honoring.

The English instructor is not just teaching English—she is liberating people from the natural things of this world that keep them in bondage. Liberating students from these things honors Christ. Teaching overseas can be God's instrument to set the captive free when we teach in Jesus' name, seeing that teaching our discipline from a Christian perspective *is* kingdom work.

Christian educators must integrate their faith into their academic discipline. This is vital because Christ's lordship over all of creation demands it. Willard (1999) declared that Jesus is the smartest man that ever lived:

> If we truly see him as the premier thinker of the human race—and who *else* would be that?—then we are also in a position to honor him as the most knowledgeable person in *our* field, whatever that may be, and to ask his cooperation and assistance with everything we have to do. (p. 611)

Second, Christian educators must consider how their worldview informs their teaching, classroom climate and the many messages transmitted in classroom interactions. The integration process must take place in both principle and practice, both philosophically and pedagogically (Gangel, 1983). All this is crucial because "it is important that the teacher be transparently Christian as well as an enthusiastic and careful scholar, and that he not compartmentalize the two but think integrationally himself" (Holmes, 1975, p. 83).

The Christian educator's focus is on glorifying God. Martin Luther, referring to the "I am the vine" passage in John 15:5, wrote,

There is a big difference between a believer's works and an unbeliever's works—even if they do the exact same thing. For an

---

Bill B., J.D., Constitutional Law, the former Soviet Union

Many years ago, before an invitation to teach law overseas came, I was studying the questions: What is conflict? Why do we have it? How should we behave in conflict? How can we help others who are in conflict? What is justice? How do we receive it? How can human systems deliver more of it?

In my studies, I came to a number of conclusions. Principal among them being: Without conflict, we would not need the word "justice" in our vocabulary. Justice comes from God and God alone! As a result, we should deal with conflict according to his directions—confession, forgiveness and sacrificial burden bearing.

When the invitation to teach law in the former Soviet Union came (late in 1993), our world was a conflict-filled mess. We had the first Gulf War, the disintegration of the former Soviet Union, a massive upheaval throughout the Middle East, and the designation of the U.S. as "The Great Satan" by extremists. We had also come, in my opinion, to a time when the principal exports of the U.S. were consumerism and "democracy without responsibility." This was a result of what others saw when looking inside the U.S. from the outside—personal liberty run wild and the universal moral law being trodden underfoot.

The invitation to me was very specific: "Russia wants someone to come and teach the words and practices of Western law along with its biblical underpinnings because they, of all people, know that without a moral underpinning, law is meaningless."

---

unbeliever's works don't spring from the vine—Jesus. That's why unbelievers cannot please God. Their works are not Christian fruit. But because a believer's works come from faith in Christ, they are all genuine fruit. (Luther/Galvin, 1998, 24:231)

If Luther is right, then there should be a difference between a believer's way of teaching and that of a nonbeliever. Because there is no dichotomy of sacred and secular for the believer, the Christian educa-

---

Over the years, I have developed three areas where I feel I can effectively communicate this and do what I've been hired to do:

1. Outlining the great divide in development of law between the West and East, while showing the Judeo-Christian and other philosophical underpinnings of Western law and presenting the "how we do law—the good, bad and ugly" juxtapositioned with a biblical process of dealing with conflict.
2. What does rule of law look like under a constitution?
3. How to listen to a question exposing a fundamental ache of heart and respond to it with gentleness and reverence from the biblical perspective of conflict, law, justice and government.

So why now, after fifteen years, aging and in not-so-good health, do I still come alive when I get on a plane to go and do it again? How could I not take an opportunity to introduce those whom I meet to the Author of Law (God the Father), Finisher and Perfect Example of Law (Jesus of Nazareth, The Christ and Lord), and Breather of Life into the Dead Black Letter of Law (Holy Spirit)? Today the efforts of so much of the former Soviet Union to establish meaningful life without rule of law fail to satisfy the hunger of the heart. The lack of comprehension of law and justice I see in my students—now some of them are teachers of law—compels me to continue teaching biblical analysis of law, justice and living in peace. And so I go.

---

tor focuses on excellence in the classroom for the purpose of glorifying God. Christians are exhorted to do all for the glory of God, "And whatever you do, whether in word or deed, do it all in the name of the Lord Jesus, giving thanks to God the Father through him. . . . Whatever you do, work at it with all your heart, as working for the Lord, not for human masters, since you know that you will receive an inheritance from the Lord as a reward. It is the Lord Christ you are serving" (Col 3:17, 23-24).

CONCLUSION

For the believer, there is no secular world and sacred world, but a single world created by God. If a teacher's religious and ethical convictions do not shape her teaching, then what does? The Christian faith cannot be an individual, private matter that has no bearing on

Ted T., Ph.D., Cultural and Religious Studies, Czech Republic

Michaela was a student in my comparative worldviews class. When she was younger, she was heavily into tennis. She worked hard, but she often had fits of extreme anger, yelling obscenities and smashing her racquet. She finally quit, but her anger turned into self-hatred, and she tried to commit suicide several times. She told me that when she rides her scooter, she has to learn to get into the habit of wearing a helmet: "I have to become used to the idea that I don't want to die."

Her life took a turn for the better when she got involved in the "Humanist Movement," a group committed to bettering the human condition through acts of service (she's involved with children in Kenya). It helped her see past her own self-hatred. She discovered that she really does love others, and that there is some good inside her. But her atheistic upbringing left her with no spiritual resources and no reason *why* people ought to do good to each other. She was very excited to read Glenn Tinder's article "Can We Be Good Without God?" for my class, as he spoke about how human rights historically has been the day-to-day business of life. Christians must be able to compare and contrast their worldview with those held by others. Sire (1990) explains that worldview analysis

> allows one to discover and examine the underlying presuppositions of every academic theory and every discipline . . . allows Christians to identify the biblical presuppositions that can undergird proper scholarship . . . provides the basis for interdisciplinary studies. (pp. 155-57)

As Christian teachers we must be able to articulate our worldview and understand the relationship between our stated worldview and our behavior. Our instruction, decisions and actions reveal what we really believe. Students and colleagues by observation will learn what is most important in our lives. Whether we like it or not, we will

---

grounded in the Christian teaching of agape love.

Michaela is now convinced that Christianity has the answers she's looking for, but the whole idea of the existence of God and living for him is very strange to her. She knows very little about Christian spirituality. She confessed she didn't really know what I meant when I mentioned *prayer* in class. Her parents and friends think she is crazy for being interested in Christianity (this is a typical reaction; many Czechs tend to think you have to be brain-damaged to take Christianity seriously). We had lunch and I explained a little more about Christianity, sin, the cross, God's forgiveness and how the Spirit empowers us to live for God. She plans to take a break from school to travel in order to figure out what she really believes (believe me, this makes sense to a Czech). But she asked me to lend her some books to take with her when she travels to Kenya and Argentina.

Michaela is why I do what I do: to challenge people and give some answers, to clear up distorted preconceptions about Christianity, and to build relationships that will lead people to Jesus. I pray for her and other students like her who need hope and answers.

Table 2

	Your Christian Worldview	The Worldview of the Culture Where You Will Be Teaching
What is the cause of evil and suffering in society?		
Do all individuals in society have the same rights to food, shelter, education and medical care?		
Is the individual more important than society, or society more important than the individual?		
Why does poverty exist?		
Is a classless society desirable?		
Should men and women be treated equally?		
Does an individual's identity continue after death?		
What do you think about paying a dowry before marriage?		
What do you think of arranged marriages?		

influence students' and colleagues' lives.

Stott (1972) points out that God created "thinking beings; he has treated us as such by communicating with us in words; he has renewed us in Christ and given us the mind of Christ; and he will hold us responsible for the knowledge we have" (p. 26). Our goal is to develop a Christian worldview from which a Christian philosophy of education can be extracted. The purpose of having a biblical faith and worldview is not simply to comfort believers but to transform the world. We must realize that "the way we see the world can change the world" (Colson, 1999, p. 13).

Christian educators are called to transform the thinking of students so they begin to see the world from a Christian viewpoint. Therefore let us be diligent about developing a solid and mature biblical worldview, with consistency in our private lives and at the blackboard. Teaching as a Christian mission focuses on excellence and Christlike behavior so that our influence both inside and outside the classroom might move others toward the Savior. In the end, it is not what we say we believe, but it is our decisions, actions and attitudes that reveal who we really are, what we really believe, and the basis of our worldview.

GOING DEEPER, GOING FURTHER

Questions to Consider

1. What aspects of your personal history shape how you understand the world and the classroom?

2. What are some ways that "being an American" has shaped your understanding of the world?

3. In which areas of your worldview do you think you most likely share common ground with students in your class, and in which areas do you think you are more likely to differ?

4. How can these similarities aid in your teaching? How might these differences hamper teaching effectiveness?

Exercise/Activities to Engage

Worldviews are very complex and changing. The chart on page 52 is a brief exercise that provides you with an opportunity to consider your Christian worldview but also the worldview held by many of the people you will be interacting with and teaching. Use the Internet and readings to complete the chart as best as you can. Support your positions with Scripture.

Suggested Reading List

Books

Naming the Elephant: Worldview as a Concept, James Sire

The Outrageous Idea of Christian Scholarship, George Marsden

The Universe Next Door: A Basic Worldview Catalog, James Sire

Your Mind Matters: The Place of the Mind in the Christian Life, John Stott

Articles

"The Academy and Jesus," Ken Elzinga, *Faith & Economics* 37, Spring (2001): 31-35

REFERENCE LIST

Blamires, H. (2005). *The Christian mind: How should a Christian think?* Reprint. Vancouver: Regent College Publishing. (Originally published 1963).

Colson, C., & Pearcey, N. (1999). *How now shall we live?* Wheaton, IL: Tyndale House Publishers.

Dovring, K. (1997). *English as lingua franca: Double talk in global persuasion.* Westport, CT: Praeger.

Gaebelein, F. E. (1968). *The pattern of God's truth: Problems of integration in Christian education.* Chicago: Moody Press.

Gangel, K. O. (1983). *Toward a harmony of faith and learning: Essays on Bible college curriculum.* Famington Hills, MI: William Tyndale College Press.

Giroux, H. A., & McLaren, P. (1996). Teacher education and the politics of engagement: The case for democratic schooling. In P. Leistyna, A. Woodrum & S. A. Sherblom (Eds.), *Breaking free:*

The transformative power of critical pedagogy, (pp. 301-31). Cambridge, MA: Harvard University Press.

Hasker, W. (1992). Faith-learning integration: An overview. *Christian Scholars Review, 21*(3), 231-48.

Holmes, A. F. (1975). *The idea of a Christian college.* Grand Rapids: Eerdmans.

Lewis, C. S. (1996). *The abolition of man.* (5th ed.). New York: Touchstone. (Originally published 1944).

Luther, M. (1998). *By faith alone.* Grand Rapids: World Publishing (Gen. Ed. James C. Galvin).

Oakes, J., & Lipton, M. (1999). *Teaching to change the world.* Boston: McGraw-Hill.

Palmer, P. (1998). *The courage to teach: Exploring the inner landscape of a teacher's life.* San Francisco: Jossey-Bass.

Purpel, D. E. (1989, Spring). *The moral and spiritual crisis in education.* Granby, MA: Bergin & Garvey.

Romanowski, M. H. (1998). Teachers' lives and beliefs: Influences that shape the U.S. history curriculum. *Mid-Western Educational Researcher, 11*(2), 2-8.

Sire, J. W. (1990). *Discipleship of the mind: Learning to love God in the ways we think.* Downers Grove, IL: InterVarsity Press.

Sire, J. W. (2004). *Naming the elephant: Worldview as a concept.* Downers Grove, IL: InterVarsity Press.

Snow, D. (2000). *English teaching as Christian mission: An applied theology.* Scottdale, PA: Herald Press.

Stott, J. R. W. (1972). *Your mind matters.* Downers Grove, IL: InterVarsity Press.

Vanden Berg, F. (1978). *Abraham Kuyper.* Grand Rapids: Eerdmans.

Walsh, B. J., & Middleton, J. R. (1984). *The transforming vision: Shaping a Christian worldview.* Downers Grove, IL: InterVarsity Press.

Willard, D. (1999). Jesus the logician. *Christian Scholar's Review, 28*(4), 605-14.

3

Philosophy of
Education 101

Once when Mike was teaching educational philosophy in an undergraduate class in the U.S., a student piped up and said, "I'm not sure why I need to know about philosophy and all this stuff. I just want to be a teacher and help kids." Mike was about to blow a gasket and intensely challenge this remark when he realized that this perspective was not far from what some of his own university colleagues believed. In fact, the student voiced what many teachers around the world think: "Philosophy of education isn't really relevant to me or my teaching." But they're wrong.

A philosophy of education plays a tremendous role in what happens in the classroom. A teacher's philosophy of education, whether she realizes it or not, is her guiding compass. It is the plumb line for all she does. It steers her when she is designing a course syllabus, setting goals and objectives; it directs her as she designs examinations and homework assignments. She may not even be aware that she has a philosophy of education, but it's influencing the *way* she teaches, *what* she teaches and *how* she responds to students. Even Mike's student was stating his true philosophy of education when he said "I just want to help kids." That is a part of educational philosophy; it deals with education's purposes—to help children. That student's desire to help children is a guiding belief that will impact his classroom teaching.

For those teaching crossculturally there are two main reasons for having a well-formed philosophy of education. First, a philosophy of education helps us discern clear goals, what materials are vital and what topics need to be covered. It guides us in teaching, lesson plans, relationships with students, grading, curriculum and textbook choices. Second, all teachers, no matter how experienced, will face new and unfamiliar challenges in another culture, and some of their presuppositions and approaches to teaching simply will not work. By having a clearly stated philosophy of education, a teacher in a crosscultural classroom can more easily discern what conflicts and/or what fits with the host culture and make necessary adjustments.

This chapter addresses the questions "What is a philosophy of education?" and "How do I form one?" Our goal is to help you understand and develop a philosophy of education from a distinctly Christian perspective.

THINKING ABOUT PHILOSOPHY OF EDUCATION

Knowing educational philosophy stimulates a reflective attitude that enables teachers to learn from experiences and theory. North American culture is not very reflective. We are more concerned with pragmatic actions and results than with theory. Our concern is for the *how* and not the *why*. We often fail to realize that everything we do in the classroom has a philosophical dimension. When teachers discuss what should be included in the curriculum for a course of study or how to best teach particular information, their responses and ideas grow out of their underlying philosophical beliefs.

Teachers who grasp the importance of educational philosophy and who then reflect systematically about their practices are better equipped to improve students' learning. Their awareness enables them to better understand themselves, their teaching, their beliefs and values, and their students. They become deliberate about what

Philosophy of education is the study of questions about education and its purpose(s), the process of education, the nature of knowing and the nature of human beings. It deals with the relationship between education and society, education and culture, and education and government. A teacher's philosophy of education answers questions about the ideals of education, the teacher's role, what should be taught and by what methods.

they teach and how they present information. Understanding educational philosophy enables teachers to think more clearly and decisively about a wide range of issues. Without an understanding of educational philosophy and theory, teachers' responses are more likely to be arbitrary and short-sighted. Teachers must have a coherent theory that guides their thinking about education. Philosophy sets up the aims of education and projects ways in which teachers can meet these ends. The bottom line is that philosophy gives direction to educational practices and decisions.

In addition, educational philosophy teaches how and what to question. Philosophy enables teachers to raise critical questions. Professional educators must be able to think intelligently about issues that underlie educational practices and how their responses impact their teaching and students. Teachers must daily consider questions regarding their educational philosophy, in both words and actions, as they present knowledge and interact with students.

In the final analysis, no educational practice can proceed without a philosophy of education. Every policy or procedure is laden with assumptions of what education should be and how the goals of education should be carried out. If teachers become more aware of this, they can better assess their teaching. Thus teachers must maintain a close relationship between educational philosophy and their teaching.

For the Christian educator, philosophy of education is essential because Christianity and the philosophy of education address the same basic questions: the meaning of life, morality and the value of knowledge. How you answer these questions forms a distinct point of view and influences education.

PHILOSOPHY OF EDUCATION AND CULTURE

Philosophy of education deals with three tiers of questions. The first tier tries to answer big-picture questions such as the meaning of life, the human condition, the nature of reality, issues of right and wrong, and even the existence of God. The second tier responds to the first by looking at issues such as the role of government in education, political influences, social and economic structures, and beliefs about gender and human rights. When those questions are dealt with and definitive answers are formulated, the third tier moves to pragmatic aspects of teaching. It asks questions such as "What should be

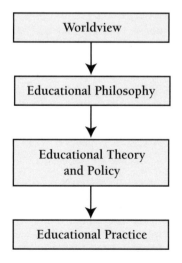

Figure 2. (Adapted from Peterson, 1986.)

taught?" and "What is the role of the teacher?" and deals with approaches to learning, assessment and overall goals of education.

This may sound overly theoretical, but worlds can clash in an overseas classroom when a teacher enters from another culture and worldview and tries to apply his own teaching techniques. A society's philosophy of education is birthed out of that culture's worldview and what it values most. Then from that educational philosophy come policy and ultimately classroom practice. Figure 2 diagrams the progression from worldview to educational practice.

Let's look at some examples of how philosophy of education is influenced by governments' ideology and culture.

The former Soviet Union's worldview was based on socialist ideals. One of the primary aspects of this worldview was that peasants (farmers) were the backbone of a workers' proletarian society. As a result, a month of potato picking on communal farms was incorporated into the sophomore college curriculum. Every sophomore in every university across the Soviet Union knew that the month of October was devoted to picking potatoes. Classes were cancelled, and they were not allowed to go home for that month. They packed a small bag of belongings and off they went to live with "Farmer Cherkovsky." The purpose of this exercise was to reinforce into every privileged university sophomore the realization that farm work was hard and noble. Citizens of a great communist country should never lose sight of that fact. The government's worldview influenced the philosophy of education which then influenced classroom practice. Worldview: Peasantry is the backbone of a socialist system. Philosophy of education: Peasantry should not be forgotten by students. Classroom practice: Students pick potatoes to reconnect with the peasantry.

One communist nation in Asia executed criminals every six months in the public square. The government required all high school and university students to attend these public executions in cities and towns across the nation. The communist regime wanted to reinforce to its citizenry that crime was not tolerated. Part of their worldview as a communist totalitarian government was to impart fear to their citizens—fear of breaking any law or going against the government. This worldview of governing shaped the nation's philosophy of education, which in turn showed up in classroom practice. So young impressionable college and high school students were required to view an execution as a part of the national curriculum, reminding them that the government was in control. Although public executions were done away with by 1985, this principle is still a vital part of this nation's philosophy of education today. Worldview: Society needs a totalitarian system to survive. Philosophy of education: Students must be taught that government is always to be obeyed. Classroom practice: Expose students to the consequences of disobeying the government.

Students in the Islamic nation of Afghanistan are raised to have respect for their elders and those in authority. Because of this, students wholeheartedly believe that teachers are their superiors. As a result, students in Afghanistan must stand in class when asking or answering a question to show respect for their teachers. Worldview: One's elders are to be treated with the utmost respect. Philosophy of education: Part of education is to teach students to respect their elders. Classroom practice: A student must always stand when asking or answering a question of the teacher.

A nation's worldview has a tremendous impact on what takes place in the classroom. When we teach in a distant classroom, our effectiveness depends on knowing as much as possible about the host nation's philosophy of education and having a well-formed one of our own. When Teri taught in China she initially believed that as a teacher she needed to walk around the classroom, moving among the students to make connections and to hold their attention. She had always been taught that way. In fact, her favorite teachers were those who didn't stay behind a desk but were hands-on and interacted physically with the students. (Her philosophy of education was informing her beliefs about the role of the teacher and how students learn.) Little did she know that her students were completely unable

William W., Ph.D., Christianity and Comparative Religions, Asia

I team taught Judaism and Christianity with a Chinese professor who occasionally translated technical terms or unfamiliar concepts for me in class. He is a member of the Communist Party and admits that he does not embrace my worldview. I was shocked when he suggested that I tell my Western friends, "If they want to see the effects of sin, tell them to come here. Everyone here does as he pleases with no thought for others. I wish everyone would become a real Christian." Despite his atheistic ideological background, he enthusiastically supports my work.

to learn because they were so uncomfortable with their teacher roaming around the classroom.

When she realized she wasn't connecting with the students and saw the frightened looks on their faces, she asked if she might observe a Chinese colleague's class. There she learned that the teacher never leaves the lectern or moves from behind the desk and doesn't make physical contact with students. What Teri believed to be a good teaching practice was actually hindering students' learning. Her underlying American philosophy of education didn't work in her Chinese classroom experience.

The Chinese philosophy of education is based on examinations. Students are taught by rote and memorization in order to pass a series of exams throughout their educational careers. This focus on the teacher's giving students information and knowledge to memorize for the exam is called "duck stuffing" by Chinese educators. The practice fills students with all the necessary facts and figures so that at the national examinations they can regurgitate the information and pass the exam. Duck-stuffing philosophy doesn't leave room for creative thinking or problem-solving skills. But Teri's internal philosophy of education cried out that students need critical thinking skills for the twenty-first-century global community. She had to reformulate her purposes and goals and teach in a way that students could receive it.

So she gradually weaned her students from duck stuffing by explaining to them that classroom practices were going to look a little different in her classroom. Carefully, and always with clear explanations, Teri brought her students into a less teacher-centered classroom, into a more student-centered environment. In order to do this, she had to know what her purposes were, where she was going, and what she wanted the students to be able to do when the class was over. All of this is philosophy of education in practice.

DEVELOPING A PHILOSOPHY OF EDUCATION

Developing a philosophy of education allows teachers to become familiar with the major questions of education. It helps them think through these questions and begin to steer their thinking toward the classroom. When a teacher considers these questions and is able to answer them, the task is to take the "theoretical" answers and move them into classroom practices. This is what Teri had to work through in China. These are the questions she and all teachers need to ask to form a philosophy of education:

1. What is the basis of knowledge and truth?

2. What are the purposes, aims and goals of education?

3. How should teachers view their students?

4. What should make up the curriculum content, and how should it be organized?

5. What role should academics and spiritual/moral growth of the student play in education?

6. What is the nature and role of the teacher?

7. What approaches to teaching should be used?

8. What are the roles of government in education?

9. What are the roles of parents in education?

10. What are the roles of students in education?

Epistemology **is** **the** **branch** **of** **philosophy** **that** **studies** **the** **nature** **and** **scope** **of** **knowledge.** **It** **is** **the** **theory** **of** **knowing** **and** **knowledge.** **It** **centers** **on** **notions** **of** **truth** **and** **belief.** **Epistemologists** **examine** **the** **justifications** **for** **knowledge** **claims.** **Epistemology** **asks,** **"Do** **you** **really** **know** **what** **you** **think** **you** **know?"** **and** **if** **so,** **"How** **do** **you** **know** **what** **you** **know?"**

These seemingly theoretical questions actually force us to articulate and plan for the basic outcomes of education. When a philosophy of education is intentionally defined, educators can then select the aims of education and effectively choose course content as well as teaching methods (or techniques) to promote them. Every educational philosophy has to encounter the hard realities of the classroom—it stands or falls according to the human experience. That's true for all classrooms around the world.

KNOWLEDGE AND TEACHING

Education by its very nature is intended to develop "knowing" of some kind. The foundation of education is an understanding of the nature and scope of knowledge. Because of this, epistemology is of pressing interest to educators and plays a major role in developing an educational philosophy. Epistemology attempts to answer the questions of knowledge.

- What is truth?
- What are the sources of knowledge?
- How is knowledge determined?
- What does it mean to know?
- How may knowing be promoted?
- How are knowledge claims derived? From divine revelation, logic, intuition, empirical evidence or subjective personal experience?

Knowledge is usually based on some type of authority, research or concepts of reality. For instance, in many Islamic nations, the Qur'an (along with the Hadith) is the authority for all knowledge. Therefore their epistemology comes from what they believe to be Qur'anic truth. The Qur'an teaches that women are deficient in intelligence (Hadith 1:181-82) and that two women are equal in value to one man. This is evidenced in their courts by the fact that a woman's testimony is worth only half that of a man's (Parshall, 1994, p. 179). Because women are not considered as intelligent as men, education for women is viewed as an inappropriate use of time and resources. Education is available to

---

Scott (and Christy) G., J.D., Law Professor, Romania

Being a missionary is like most endeavors; you have good days, bad days, and in-between days. There can be times when you wonder, "Is any of this getting through?" As in American law schools, we use the Socratic method as much as possible here. Instead of simply down-loading information into the student's head through lecturing, we try to draw out understanding through questioning. We attempt to lead students to logical conclusions through a series of questions, so they learn how to actually think for themselves. This is *not* the Romanian way, and it can be challenging at times.

However, in a class one Monday, the Socratic method was working almost too well. We were covering the concept of free will (i.e., our ability to choose good or evil) and trying to make the connection between free will and humanity's created purpose of having a "genuine love relationship with God." Scott was acknowledging the pain and suffering associated with humanity's freewill choices and expressing mock confusion as to why a sovereign God would have given us this ability. At this point, with great sincerity a student named Teodora said, "Don't you *see,* Scott? *We* could never *truly* love God if we didn't also have the ability to choose *not* to love God." It was a priceless and perfect Socratic/professor/missionary moment.

---

women in more moderate Muslim nations, but does not have the same priority as educating men. Their philosophy of education, based on their epistemology, marginalizes the education of girls.

The epistemological assumptions held by an educator and an educational system will shape pedagogical aims and methodologies because the methods of teaching and learning are closely related to "how we know." Thus if one's epistemological assumption is that knowledge and ideas are innately present in the mind, the Socratic method, based on the Greek philosopher and educator Socrates, of asking provocative questions would be the teaching strategy used to bring knowledge to consciousness. If the belief is that learning is transactional between the person and the environment, as the American educator John Dewey asserted, then the most effective teaching method is problem-solving and experience-based education (this is a hands-on approach to education). If knowledge is located in a more wise and intelligent individual (the expert), such as the belief of China based on Con-

Table 3

Western	compared to	Eastern
Linear		Cyclical
Aristotle/Socrates		Brahman monks/Confucius
Problem solving		Rote memorization
Student-centered		Teacher-centered
Task-based		Exam-based
Mentoring		Hierarchical
Pragmatic		Classical
Vocational		Historical
Discussion (dialogue/debate)		Unquestioned (accepted)
Students perceive		Students receive
Individualistic		Communal
A constant changing body of knowledge		An unchanged core body of knowledge
Sensory		Aesthetic

fucius's teaching, where the teacher dispenses this knowledge to students, then lectures only would be the method of choice.

In the West, we have been influenced by a variety of factors that have shaped our epistemological assumptions, philosophy and teaching methods. Table 3 compares and contrasts Western to Eastern approaches to knowledge and learning and illustrates how cultural factors impact teaching and learning.

Teachers in a distant classroom must not underestimate these differences. Overseas educators must know the culture in which they are teaching. They need to be aware that students bring into the classroom their own ways of knowing. Understanding students' ways of knowing will enable the educator to better teach, influence and sometimes challenge students' thinking and learning. It also helps reduce conflicts and misunderstandings both between school administrators and teacher and between student and teacher. It helps close the cultural gap between the Christian educator overseas and the students he has come to serve.

OTHER INFLUENCES ON EDUCATIONAL PHILOSOPHY

Culture influences a nation's philosophy of education. Every educational system in the world has a philosophy of education that is based in the culture, the government system and in the value system (religious and nonreligious) of that country and society. It is also influenced by worldview, political agendas and socioeconomic factors. In general the U.S. philosophy of education might resemble something like this:

> All people have the right to an education, regardless of their gender, race, religion, sexual orientation, ethnic background, socioeconomic status, physical or mental challenges, that will empower them and give them tools for vocational, social, cultural, moral, economic, psychological and physiological well-being and will develop in them outcomes necessary for living and contributing to society at all levels, including familial, governmental,

economic, societal and cultural; outcomes which can be assessed and evidenced through some type of action or result by a professionally trained and certified teacher or educator.

Based on the above description of American educational philosophy, one can easily see how this influences the public school ethos, curriculum and teaching. The belief that all people are entitled to an education renders public school free of cost. Based on this concern for equality, schools ensure that special education is available for the mentally challenged and that issues such as inclusion[1] find their way into educational discourse. Schools provide government and civic courses in order to develop "good citizens." Programs on societal problems such as teenage pregnancy and drug use are implemented in order to improve society. The strong movement toward outcome-based education has created high-stakes testing at all grade levels. Although this is a simplistic description of American education, it illustrates the impact of cultural beliefs on philosophy of education.

A nation's theology also influences its philosophy of education. For example, much of African theology, both Christian and Muslim, focuses on the supernatural aspects of God. It has a strong sense of demonic activity, spiritual warfare and supernatural manifestations. God is a God one can feel and sometimes see. It is intuitive, kept alive by oral traditions and focuses on phenomena and experience. It believes in providence, and God is a strict disciplinarian (suffering is a part of religion). Learned men of the faith are considered to have supreme authority and are never to be questioned but are to be submitted to unconditionally.

Thus African nations traditionally often have a philosophy of education that reflects their theology. Students' comfort is of little importance to the teacher. Suffering is a part of learning—learning is never to be fun or recreational. Students see teachers as supreme authorities who are never to be questioned or doubted. Oral tradi-

---

[1]Inclusion is the practice of mainstreaming kids with special needs, both physical and mental, into regular classrooms for the purpose of teaching tolerance and acceptance as well as challenging students.

tions and narratives play a major role in the classroom, in part due to the lack of textbooks, but also because of cultural norms. Bad grades can be seen as a result of laziness, which might be due to the influence of demons or other supernatural factors. God is a God one can feel; therefore education is not based exclusively on facts and scientific information, but also on intuition, personal experiences and folklore. The student/teacher relationship in most African nations is based on tribal traditions, and students often call their instructors Father or Mother.

Although culture and theology will impact our individual philosophies of education to varying degrees, as Christians we must consider the questions raised earlier in this chapter as we construct a Christian philosophy of education. Culture impacts national philosophy and worldview. It trickles down to shape the philosophy of education that operates in every classroom around the world. As an educator teaching overseas, you too have cultural priorities ingrained in you, some that you may not even be aware of. Your philosophy of education will manifest itself in your reactions to:

Life in the Classroom

- Cheating
- Turning papers in late
- Discussion in the classroom (Q&A exercises)
- The role of gender
- The teacher-student relationship
- Expectations of students
- Class and semester schedules
- Class rosters
- Classroom management
- Examinations

Life in the Department

- Relationships (the department chair, colleagues, administrative clerical workers)

- Departmental meetings

- Dealing with overworked, underpaid colleagues

Life in the Culture

- Your perception of history

- Your belief in absolutes

- Your understanding of human rights

- An individualistic approach versus a communal approach

- Belief that human beings should have control over their environment

These are all a part of one's philosophy of education and a vital part of a Christian philosophy of education. The key for the Christian educator is to develop sound responses to these various educational issues that reflect a biblical perspective.

A CHRISTIAN PHILOSOPHY
OF EDUCATION AT THE BLACKBOARD

How does a Christian teacher develop a sound philosophy of education? As Christians we need to examine our presuppositions about teaching and learning from Scripture and Christ's example instead of drawing exclusively from contemporary philosophical thought. Not all secular educational philosophy should be cast aside by Christian educators. Rather, Christian educators must view these philosophies in light of a Scipture and determine which elements are compatible with the Christian mind and which are not. Philosophical analysis is required in order to filter each concept or idea to uncover its fundamental beliefs and assumptions. Then we must determine if the components are compatible with a Christian worldview.

The question that now surfaces is "What kinds of teaching will enable a Christian teacher to work with maximum continuity between her teaching and her faith, as one working before the face of God?" (Smith, 1993, p. 37). What are the probing questions that Christian educators must consider as they integrate their Christian faith at the blackboard? Adding to the basic list of questions given earlier, we must also ask:

1. From a biblical perspective, what basic skills should education cultivate in students?

2. How do Christian teachers nurture students in a Christ-honoring way?

3. What do biblical truths tell us about learning and teaching?

4. From a biblical perspective, what is the nature and role of the teacher?

5. What does the Bible say about educational methods such as discovery, demonstration and involvement of students?

6. Is there a biblical perspective of lectures, memorization, critical thinking, small group activities, visuals, question-and-answer—the very things that make up methodology?

7. Is there a biblical perspective on assessment (grading)? Should grading be subjective, objective, test-taking, group assessment, formative and/or summative?

In addition, we must look at the field we are teaching—our actual discipline and how it fits into a Christian worldview. Hasker (1992) provides four major dimensions of integration in the theoretical disciplines. First, Christians must ask questions regarding what fundamental insights and convictions, derivable from the Christian worldview, are relevant to the discipline.

Second, Christians must consider disciplinary foundations. These are foundational assumptions such as methodological and epistemological issues that are the very basis of the discipline. The Christian must ask whether these are particularly significant or problematic from the standpoint of the Christian faith.

Third, disciplinary practice is concerned with issues that arise in the day-to-day practice of actually doing one's job as a historian, physicist or teacher. Within this dimension there are concerns about ethics, values and attitudes.

Finally, Hasker asks what specific contribution this discipline makes to the Christian vision of reality. Hasker challenges Christians to investigate how this discipline furthers the kingdom of God.

Based on the above discussion and listed questions, the following serves an example of how a teacher's faith in Christ informs both the theoretical and practical aspects of his or her pedagogy.

Question:

How should teachers view students?

Biblical responses:

- All human beings have value because they are made in the image of God.

- Because all human beings are valuable they should be treated with respect and dignity.

- Humans have an innate tendency to seek knowledge and understanding. Teachers must find and utilize this tendency, focusing on relevant and interesting lessons.

- God created human beings with different personalities and different approaches to learning.

Biblical responses put into educational practice:

- Students are treated with respect, and classroom management strategies must be based on respect. Students are never humiliated, never gossiped about to others, and all are treated fairly. Create positive teacher-students interaction.

- Educators must incorporate different teaching strategies in order to engage students with different learning styles.
- Teachers must respect students as individuals and set appropriate expectations.

These are just a few of the countless issues and questions that need to be asked by all Christian educators. We use these to illustrate how a Christian philosophy of education is developed and placed into practice. In particular, the question of the nature and role of the teacher has implications for modeling, creating classroom climate, knowledge of academic areas, communication skills, developing environments favorable for learning, issues of classroom management, the role of motivation and assessment techniques.

This is the beginning of the development of a Christian philosophy of education. There are many possible responses to educational issues that are solidly based on a biblical perspective. Our worldview and educational philosophy, just like our pedagogy, is always a work in progress—changing, adapting, growing stronger and more mature as we experience life, the classroom and our walk with the Lord. It is important for us as teachers to identify the underpinnings of our classroom practice because teaching directly and indirectly impacts the lives of our students. Maintaining consistency between theory and practice is the essence of good teaching. Therefore teachers must consciously understand what they believe and how that shapes pedagogical decisions.

CONCLUSION

All teachers must understand the role worldviews, educational philosophy and theory play in teaching. No teacher can escape these influences, so it is essential for all teachers to work out their worldviews and educational philosophies. It is imperative to reflect, rethink and reconsider the implications for their teaching and students. They need to be aware of what they believe about life and teaching. Also they must learn the skill of philosophical

Glen T., Ph.D., Comparative Religions, Central Asia

On my first day lecturing at the national university, I entered the office of the chair of the philosophy department a half hour before class was to start. After welcoming me warmly with greetings and smiles, he sat down with me for the customary cup of tea. The chair immediately became serious. Dropping his head a bit and lowering his voice he said, "Dr. T, you and I have serious work to do. We must find a bridge between East and West, between Christians and Muslims. We need to find a key in order to develop mutual understanding. The key is Abraham. He is the father of the three monotheistic religions." He broke off and rose from his chair. Turning to his bookcase he reached for a book. He brought it back to the desk and opened it. Turning to the beginning he found Genesis 12:3. Then he began, "Here in the book of Genesis it says that through Abraham all the families of the earth will be blessed. This is the key."

I couldn't believe my ears. I hardly knew this Muslim man, whose father had been a mullah. So quickly he hit the mark that I aim for with my Muslim friends but so often do not hit, or at least take so long to get to this point. He continued, "Dr. T, we must write a book together. You write from the Christian point of view and I will write from the Muslim point of view. We must explain fully the meaning of the blessing of Abraham for our people so that we can learn how to live in peace and mutual understanding."

With a mixture of joy and surprise I said, "I agree, and I think that a project like this will be a benefit to many people. You are right, the blessing of Abraham is the key." Since that time we have been working on different parts of the book, and have regular conversations about the transformation that Jesus brings to those who want to seek him.

analysis that questions basic assumptions, beliefs, values, theories, methods and knowledge. This forces teachers to begin to disassemble their own multifaceted understandings of education and educational jargon and begin to convert this new self-knowledge into meaningful terms that can be articulated in consistent and effective classroom practice.

For Christian educators this is a challenging task. We must become experts in asking philosophical questions and develop sound answers from a biblical perspective. But it is a task well worth the effort. For the Christian educator teaching in a distant land, it is crucial to teach, live and relate to others decisively, consciously and purposefully in order to bring glory to Christ and to honor him in the place to which he has called you—the overseas classroom.

GOING DEEPER, GOING FURTHER

A Philosophy of Education Template
The purpose(s) of education should be to:

The values that should be taught through education are:

Students learn best when they are taught under certain conditions and in an environment that promotes learning. Developing these, teachers must:

The curriculum of any classroom should include certain "basics" that contribute to students' social, emotional, intellectual, spiritual, moral and physical development. These basics are:

The outcomes of an educational system should be:

Upon graduation from a university a student should be able to:

These goals are accomplished through:

Qualities I think are important for teachers:

Questions to Consider

1. Based on the brief comparison and contrast of Western and Eastern approaches to knowledge and learning on page 66, list several practical ways that you can adapt your teaching to meet the needs of Eastern learners.

2. List five of your fundamental beliefs about teaching and learning. How are these currently played out in your teaching? How could you defend these as being based on a sound Christian philosophy of education?

3. What is the role of the Christian teacher?

4. List five "things" you want your students to learn while in your class. How can you best accomplish this?

5. How will your beliefs affect your teaching? Think in terms of these areas:

- Classroom management
- Instructional strategies
- Teacher/student relationships
- Assessment

Suggested Reading List

Christ and Culture, Richard Niebuhr

"A Christian Perspective on John Dewey," Werner Lumm, available at http://www.bjupress.com/resourcesarticlesbalance/a-christian -perspective-on-john-dewey.php

A Christian Philosophy of Education, Gordon Clark

The Christian Philosophy of Education Explained, Stephen Perk (this is
a heavy read with very technical vocabulary)

*Democracy and Education: An Introduction to the Philosophy of Educa-
tion,* John Dewey (secular)

Philosophy of Education: Issues and Options, Michael Peterson

*Philosophy of Education: Studies in Philosophies, Schooling, and Educa-
tional Polices,* Edward Power (secular)

Questions That Matter: An Invitation to Philosophy, Ed Miller (secular)

What Is Education? E. C. Moore

With All Your Mind: A Christian Philosophy of Education, Michael
Peterson

Women's Ways of Knowing: The Development of Self, Voice and Mind,
Mary Belenky et al. (secular)

REFERENCE LIST

The Hadith, Sahih Bukhari ed.

Hasker, W. (1992). Faith-learning integration: An overview. *Christian
Scholar's Review, 21*(3), 231-48.

Parshall, P. (1994). *Understanding Muslim teachings and traditions.*
Grand Rapids: Baker Books.

Peterson, M. L. (1986). *Philosophy of education: Issues and options.*
Downers Grove, IL: InterVarsity Press.

Smith, D. (1993). Can modern language teaching be Christian? *Spec-
trum, 25*(1), 25-38.

4

Curriculum Shmurriculum

Who Needs This?

When Teri taught English as a Foreign Language (EFL) in China she took with her a prepackaged EFL curriculum from the United States. It was selected by her missions-sending organization and consisted of audio tapes, a workbook, an EFL reader and a video series. The prepackaged curriculum was easy to use, gave clear help for lesson plans and chronologically guided both student and teacher through two semesters of English language learning. The lessons provided solid exercises in grammar tenses, sentence structure and syntax. The course taught students how to ask and answer questions and gave them opportunities to apply their learning through role-playing, writing and outside reading.

However, Teri began to realize that English language wasn't the only thing being taught in the materials. For example, one lesson focused on astrology and how to read one's horoscope. This lesson included a writing exercise where students were asked to write a horoscope for a specific astrological sign. Another lesson taught students how to remove themselves from conversations with people to whom they didn't want to talk. In this lesson a young man, new to the city, was trying to pry himself away from an elderly woman who wanted to make conversation with him on the city bus. A third lesson was on dating—how to ask someone on a date, how to end the date, and "to kiss or not to kiss."

When this prepackaged curriculum was taught in Chinese classrooms, powerful messages, values and beliefs were communicated to students. It taught students astrology is acceptable and legitimate. The students were shocked that the curriculum taught that Americans have little respect for the elderly. In China at that time, university students were not allowed to date, so the lesson on dating confirmed their stereotypes that the Western world was indeed promiscuous. Although the curriculum was designed to teach English, a whole lot of other things were being taught as well.

CURRICULUM SHMURRICULUM!

Curriculum is not just mathematics, English, social studies and science. It's not just a course of study or a plan for what should be taught. It is definitely not irrelevant! Curriculum is at the core of the teaching task because it influences everything we say and do in the classroom, either directly or indirectly, explicitly or implicitly. If you think curriculum is irrelevant, then you will convey messages in the classroom you never intended. The prepackaged curriculum Teri took to China taught values and beliefs she not only disagreed with, but strongly disapproved of. If you want to teach values, ethics, morals and beliefs that are in alignment with your worldview, then you will have to take time to ask, "What am I teaching?"

In this chapter we will explore how three forms of curriculum play a role in the teaching/learning process. We will discuss why Christian educators should think Christianly about all three types of curriculum and how curriculum can influence students with values and ethics honoring to Christ. We will see how the three forms of curriculum are never isolated, but always interact with each other and send messages to students.

HOW DO YOU DEFINE CURRICULUM?

Curriculum can best be defined as the materials and resources that are used as part of formal instruction of the educational experience. It may refer to textbooks, films and all other supportive teaching materials that are chosen to support the intentional instructional agenda of a teacher. Elliot Eisner (1985) points out that

> schools teach much more—and much less—than they intend to teach. Although much of what is taught is explicit and public, a great deal is not. Indeed, it is my claim that schools provide not *one* curriculum to students, but *three*. (p. 87)

The three forms of curriculum Eisner refers to are the *formal, hidden* and *null*. As teachers, we must be concerned about what our students learn from the curriculum. We need to be aware of the curriculum and resource content and what values they present to students. As educators teaching in a distant classroom, we must look at curricula with a critical eye and systematically evaluate and analyze the materials, asking, "Is this what I want to teach? Is this what I want my students to learn?"

THE FORMAL CURRICULUM

The formal curriculum is the knowledge that is deliberately and consciously dispensed in the classroom through various resources and materials. It is the knowledge that teachers want their students to learn, and students are usually held accountable for it through some form of assessment, such as tests, homework or research papers.

Teri's curriculum experience in China shows how teachers can be snared by the assumption that the formal curriculum consists of neutral and objective knowledge. Don't be misled; the formal curriculum often appears objective, but in reality the formal curriculum is anything but value-free. All knowledge presented in the classroom or "acquired in school, or anywhere for that matter—is never neutral or objective but is ordered and structured in particular ways" (McLaren, 1998, p. 169). The way knowledge is structured and presented significantly shapes the way students understand the topic, the content and the subject (like devaluing the elderly or kissing on the first date).

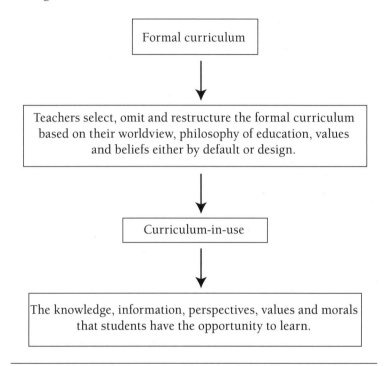

Figure 3. Formal curriculum and curriculum-in-use

So even though the formal curriculum consists of what is found in textbooks and additional materials, teachers must be intentional about reinforcing or refuting the content of the formal curriculum. Once a teacher has determined how she is going to teach the curriculum, it is called the *curriculum-in-use*. The curriculum-in-use is filtered through a teacher's worldview and her philosophy of education (see figure 3).

As Christian educators, we must purposefully transform the formal curriculum based on our biblical values and beliefs. Teachers select, omit and restructure the curriculum content according to their worldviews. So Christian educators should understand the filter they use to create the curriculum-in-use because this is where students are more apt to be shaped and influenced. In order to present a Christian (explicit or implicit) perspective to students, teachers must deliberately evaluate and transform the formal curriculum into the curriculum-in-use.

In 2005, Japanese history textbooks were criticized for whitewashing wartime atrocities, deemphasizing the abuse of Chinese and Korean women for amusement of soldiers, and sanitizing their reporting of World War II wartime events (Saaler, 2005). These textbooks are the formal curriculum. If left unquestioned and taught as-is by teachers, the textbook version of history will shape how Japanese students view their government, their nation's history and Japan's military role in WWII. However, Japanese teachers could challenge the textbook and present a different perspective by introducing additional information and materials, thus raising questions that allow students to critically evaluate the text. Then students may receive a completely different view of Japanese history. Teachers and their worldviews play a powerful role in the formal curriculum by transforming the formal curriculum into the curriculum-in-use. Christian educators must screen and evaluate the materials that they use through the lens of a Christian worldview and asking, "What is true?"

THE HIDDEN CURRICULUM

The *hidden curriculum* is perhaps even more central than the formal curriculum in developing a critical understanding of teaching. The hidden curriculum highlights the fact that students learn much more than is presented in the formal curriculum. In contrast to the formal curriculum that is designed to produce intended outcomes, the "hidden curriculum refers to the unintended outcomes of the schooling process" (McLaren, 1998, p. 186). Giroux (1983) defines hidden curriculum as "those unstated norms, values, and beliefs embedded in and transmitted to students through the underlying rules that structure the routines and social relationships in school and classroom life"

(p. 47). The hidden curriculum includes the many messages, norms and values that are transmitted daily by the formal curriculum, rules, regulations, rituals, school structure and everyday interactions.

How should a Christian educator relate to the hidden curriculum? First, know that the hidden curriculum may include both positive and negative messages that are covertly sent to students through the examples, case studies and content provided. For example, when Teri was using her Western EFL curriculum in China, if she omitted any discussion on the disrespect of the elderly or ignored it, the hidden curriculum (or message sent to students) would have been that she endorsed this behavior. She had to be proactive in explaining to students not everyone in the United States responds that way to the elderly. She had to intercept the hidden message and transform it into the curriculum-in-use.

Second, understand that role modeling, interactions with students, comments made in class, your expectations, your teaching strategies, your body language, your lifestyle, who you are—all this is hidden curriculum. Christians who are to model Christ in the classroom must be aware of how the hidden curriculum impacts students. Actions speak louder than words—that's how the hidden curriculum works.

So how should Christian educators creatively utilize the formal and hidden curricula? The key is first for teachers to thoroughly understand the curriculum that will be used in class. Second, they need to evaluate the curriculum in order to draw out elements that they find problematic from a Christian worldview. Third, these problematic elements must be transformed into the curriculum-in-use to reflect a Christian worldview and the values and beliefs teachers deem important for students to learn. Finally, they must consider the interactions with the curriculum and students and examine the messages being transmitted so they are able to remove or reinforce the messages being sent to students in order to correct, modify, enhance or explain ideas that are consistent with a Christian worldview and educational philosophy.

For example, Teri's worldview conflicted with the lesson on astrology. So she isolated and analyzed the problematic material and intentionally reworked it so that her presentation called into question the legitimacy of astrology. Then she could present the lesson to students with a clear conscience knowing that wrong or inappropriate messages had been removed or at least challenged.

Here is a list of questions that can be used to evaluate curriculum. Of course each discipline requires that educators apply their academic expertise from a Christian worldview and ask content-relevant questions.

Hidden Curriculum Questions

1. What value messages are embedded in the curriculum materials and resources that I am using?

2. What perspectives are being highlighted in the curriculum materials?

3. What perspectives are omitted?

4. Are these materials culturally relevant?

5. Are stereotypes and prejudices being presented?

6. What are the assumptions upon which the curriculum is based?

7. How well do the provided exercises and activities promote thinking?

8. Do the materials support my educational and moral goals for students?

THE NULL CURRICULUM
WHAT YOU DON'T KNOW CAN HURT YOU

The null curriculum is the knowledge and information that is omitted (Eisner, 1985). It consists of the knowledge, beliefs, values and perspectives excluded from the formal curriculum. Possible reasons for the omission might be a political agenda, prejudice, deliberate distortion or simply an oversight. Eisner proposes that what schools *do not teach* may be as important as what they *do teach*. He asserts that the knowledge students cannot or do not consider has consequences for the kinds of lives they lead. The knowledge that is omitted affects students because it limits the perspectives from which they can view particular problems, events or situations.

It also hinders the discovery of truth and facts. Perhaps most importantly, it prevents them from learning from others' mistakes. As in the case of the Japanese history textbooks, as much was being taught by what was omitted as by what was stated. When certain subjects or topics are omitted from the formal curriculum, schools and teachers are sending powerful messages to students that this content, this perspective and this skill set are not important enough to examine or develop, much less mention.

How should teachers deal with the null curriculum in the foreign classroom? First we must identify what makes up the null curriculum. Then teachers must consider the questions of who, what, why, when, where and how when they include aspects of the null curriculum into their teaching. These questions will help a teacher identify what should be changed in the null curriculum of the foreign classroom.

Null Curriculum Questions

1. How is this issue relevant to the course content? (This is very important.)

2. Will the knowledge that I present offend students and colleagues?

3. How will I introduce knowledge that needs to be addressed but may seem "controversial" or on the fringes of accepted knowledge in the culture?

4. If I choose to, how can I slowly introduce differing perspectives?

5. How can I link this perspective to students' prior knowledge and cultural backgrounds?

6. Why am I raising this issue or legitimizing this knowledge?

7. What do I want to accomplish? Am I setting long-term or short-term goals?

8. What types of critical thinking and problem-solving skills do I want to develop in students?

9. What are my own biases? Will these prevent me from treating the subject fairly?

10. What moral messages will be or should be sent to students in this lesson?

11. Will this lesson make some students uncomfortable? If so, what can I do to relieve students' fears and demonstrate respect?

12. What possible resistance and obstacles might I face?

13. Is this knowledge worth the risks and possible consequences?

14. How will this affect my future credibility as a teacher?

STEPS IN ADAPTATION AND INTEGRATION OF THE CURRICULUM

In order to effectively restructure problematic curriculum material, teachers need to apply the following steps as they analyze and adapt specific lessons within the curriculum.

Step 1. Review all teaching material in light of the hidden curriculum questions listed on page 84.

Step 2. Ask yourself if there are lessons or values in the curriculum materials you want to challenge.

Step 3. If so, analyze the lesson in detail and target the trouble spots.

Step 4. Using the null curriculum questions, design delivery and develop lesson plans to deal with the problematic content.

Step 5.   Restructure exercises and activities provided in the curriculum according to changes you made in the lesson.

Step 6.   Assess through Q&A, written assignments, dialogues or oral reports whether students have learned the intended values and the content of the revised lesson.

Here's what it looks like in the example of the astrology lesson:

Teri reviews the prepackaged curriculum. She asks the hidden curriculum questions and discovers there are lessons and values in the materials she wants to challenge. She analyzes the lesson in detail and targets the trouble spots (steps 1-3).

Next she designs her lesson plans to deal with the problematic content. She uses the null curriculum questions and plans accordingly (step 4).

The lesson begins with her asking students if they believe in astrology—why and why not. She doesn't give her opinion yet. She responds to students' beliefs in a positive way but has mapped out how she wants to debunk astrology. Once students' voices are heard and recognized, she presents her disbelief in astrology and then lists ways that astrology can actually be harmful or detrimental to the individual.

Then she moves to the next step of restructuring the homework (exercises and activities—step 5). Students are not required to write horoscopes, but instead are challenged with a writing assignment focusing on the origins of folklore or students' ideas on what determines one's destiny or fate.

She then has a time of questions and answers to assess if students have picked up her concepts and values (step 6). She ends with EFL role-playing where students pair up and create dialogues based on cultural folklore.

DEVELOPING YOUR OWN CURRICULUM

Not every teacher will have a prepackaged curriculum. In fact many teachers going overseas will have to construct their own courses. In many cases this includes the curriculum, delivery, materials, assignments and assessment. Lack of resources is a common problem, especially in emerging nations. Regardless, all teachers need to be diligent in analyzing curriculum, including their own. The following steps will help guide teachers in the development of their own course curriculum and materials.

1. Consider your course objectives and what you want your students to learn from the formal curriculum. (For example: economic systems.)

2. Locate natural spots within the curriculum that allow for easy integration of particular values that students should learn or thinking that should be challenged. (Do economic systems have a moral obligation to provide for the poor?)

3. Set objectives for what you want to accomplish in these particular lessons. (Students should understand the larger picture of economics and develop an awareness of the poor.)

4. Design delivery and develop lesson plans that will provide these values or challenges to students. (Use case studies that give illustrations where the poor are provided for through an economic system.)

5. Develop questions and appropriate examples that will help achieve your objectives. (How can an economic system develop a way to provide for the poor?)

6. Develop an assessment assignment that gives students the opportunity to apply or think about the values presented and also provides the teacher insight into what students learned from the lesson. (Analyze economic systems that work best for providing for the poor.)

CONCLUSION

Since curriculum is fundamental to teaching, Christian educators must consider how they can utilize the three types of curriculum to introduce biblical perspectives, ideas and knowledge to their students. Christian educators must use the formal, hidden and null curricula wisely, challenging students to view the world differently, from a Christian point of view (implicitly or explicitly) so they may be able to consider this perspective among the many other viewpoints that are presented to them. The knowledge we present in class, the way it is presented and how we interact with the materials should be well thought out and intentional.

GOING DEEPER, GOING FURTHER

Questions to Consider

1. What are possible ways that you could consciously use the hidden curriculum to reflect Christ in your teaching and classroom?

2. Where are natural places to integrate or raise important Christian values in your particular field of expertise?

3. Where in the curriculum can you challenge students about what they believe or introduce them to a Christian viewpoint?

Exercise/Activities to Engage

Table 4 on page 90 is based on the section "Developing Your Own Curriculum." Keep in mind the questions raised in this chapter that deal with the hidden and null curricula.

Suggested Reading List

Curriculum: Foundations, Principles and Issues, Allan C. Ornstein and Francis P. Hunkins

"Excluding Ethical Issues From U.S. History Textbooks: 911 and the War on Terror," by Michael Romanowski in *American Secondary Education* 37, no. 2 (2009)

Ideology and Curriculum (3rd ed.), Michael W. Apple

The Integration of a Biblical Worldview into Curriculum Decisions in the Christian School, Stephen A. Stairs (D.Min. project, Grand Rapids Baptist Seminary, 2002)

"Problems of Bias in History Textbooks," by Michael Romanowski in *Social Education* 60, no. 3 (1996)

Table 4

Topic, Important Concepts and Skills	Objectives: What do you want to accomplish in this unit?	Essential Questions	Resources	Possible Places for Integration	Possible Forms of Assessment
Topic:	Objectives:	Key questions that must be raised and considered in order to achieve objectives	Key resources		
Key Concepts:	Reduce jargon and unfamiliar words/text		Culturally relevant resources		
Important Skills:					
Consider Culturally Relevant Examples, Knowledge etc.					

REFERENCE LIST

Eisner, E. (1985). *The educational imagination* (2nd ed.). New York: Macmillan.

Giroux, H. A. (1983). *Theory and resistance in education: A pedagogy for the opposition.* Hadley, MA: Bergin and Garvey.

McLaren, P. (1998). *Life in schools: An introduction to critical pedagogy in the foundations of education* (3rd ed.). White Plains, NY: Longman.

Saaler, S. (2005). *Politics, memory and public opinion: The history textbook controversy and Japanese society.* Munich: Iudicium Publishing.

5

Teaching Well
Is Teaching Good

In 1991, Mary S. went to teach English at Kiev State Pedagogical University in Ukraine. She arrived only a few days after the collapse of the Soviet Union. Within the first few weeks, she made friends with her students, colleagues and neighbors. She even had a few occasions to share her faith and love for Christ, but she was not preachy or manipulative in her witnessing.

Mary was an excellent teacher. She was always prepared for class and had a heart for her students. One of her Ukrainian colleagues, Maria, a university English professor, liked Mary and enjoyed attending her classes from time to time whenever Maria's schedule permitted. Once Christianity and faith came up with Maria. Without forcing the conversation, Mary explained the difference Christ made in her life.

One day after class, frustrated by students' exam-driven approach to learning, Mary was worried that her students weren't grasping important concepts for becoming good English teachers. She walked into the campus office and declared, "I am having a bad day!" Maria, who had just attended Mary's lecture, was in the office visiting but was sitting behind the door just out of Mary's view.

Maria surprised her as she said in a beautiful Ukrainian accent, "Mary, you have had a very *good* day." Mary thought about the uncomfortable process of getting dressed that morning without any hot running water; she remembered her struggle to get on the overcrowded, unheated bus to the university, and she thought of the frustration she felt over her students' obsession with passing national exams. But she kept these thoughts to herself and gently asked Maria, "Why do you say that?"

Maria continued, "I say that you have had a very *good* day today because while I watched you teach this morning, I decided to ask Jesus into my heart."

Mary was amazed. She had not mentioned Jesus in her lecture; she hadn't quoted the Bible or presented the Four Spiritual Laws in class. She was thrilled to hear Maria's news, but was surprised and confused by how it happened. "Maria, that's great!" Mary said. "But how did my teaching help you to do that?"

Maria explained, "You are such a good teacher. Your love for your students shows, and you have such a strong desire for them to learn. When I saw you teaching today, I looked at your love and the peace on your face and I said to God, 'I want you to be my God the way you are Mary's God.' I asked him to come into my heart."

Maria's story reminds us that *how* we teach makes a tremendous impact on others—either for good or for bad. In order for us to be an expression of God's love and truth we must teach well. Five years after Mary left Ukraine, Maria died from radiation exposure at Chernobyl. Mary's teaching well made an eternal difference in Maria's life.

In this chapter, we will see why it is vital that we teach well in order to impact the lives of our students and colleagues. We look at Jesus as the model teacher in his methods, his relationships with students, his knowledge and expertise, his servant attitude, and his earnest prayer for his students. With Jesus as our model teacher, we can better emulate him in the classroom.

HOW WOULD JESUS TEACH?

In the Gospels, Jesus is addressed as "Teacher" more than any other title (Friedeman, 1990). He is considered by diverse cultures and world religions as an excellent teacher, but many disciplines and professions lack an exact model of what Jesus would do in those fields. Though we find in Scripture that Christ prepared breakfast for his disciples, we don't know his recipe. We know that Jesus was a carpenter, but the Bible does not give a detailed explanation of how he built things.

However, Scripture does describe Jesus as a teacher. Friedeman (1990) writes, "As Christian educators we would be wise to fix our eyes upon Jesus—teacher par excellence. In him we can find our objectives, the foundation for our methodology, the working stuff of our craft" (p. 13). Friedeman goes on to say that the question for teachers who want to teach Christianly is not "What would Jesus do?" but "How would Jesus teach?"

JESUS' METHODS

Jesus used examples and illustrations from his students' daily lives to bring abstract concepts into concrete understanding. "To penetrate their reality, Jesus' words had to be simple yet challenging, touching on what they knew and bridging the way to what they needed to learn" (Friedeman, 1990, p. 167). Jesus used language that was familiar to his students and created visuals from their everyday lives. For example, in the story of the rich young ruler found in Matthew 19, Jesus responded to a young rich man who asked him what to do to inherit eternal life. Jesus said, "go, sell your possessions and give to the poor" (Mt 19:21). The young man became sad and was unwilling to do this and he left. Jesus spoke this response, leaving his disciples astonished, "I tell you the truth . . . it is easier for a camel to go through the eye of a needle than for a rich man to enter the kingdom of God" (Mt 19:23-24 NIV). Jesus used things around him (known and familiar) to explain new concepts. The disciples are confused because for them wealth is a sign of God's favor. So, if a rich guy can't get into heaven, who can? And Jesus said, "It is easier for a camel to pass through an eye of a needle than for a rich man to get into heaven." Good illustration. Now his students know that it will be really hard, if not impossible, for a rich man (who is very attached to his possessions) to get into heaven. Jesus' students got his point. Jesus used real-life objects to teach difficult-to-comprehend topics. The disciples asked, "If a rich man can't get into heaven, who can?" His illustration prompted questions and he said, "With God nothing is impossible" (see Mt 19:25-26). Lesson learned.

This becomes particularly significant in crosscultural classrooms—we must use illustrations and examples that are relevant and familiar to our students. Jesus had great insight into his students' lives. He made learning a part of their daily living.

Jesus' excellence in teaching is demonstrated in his ability to effectively teach one-on-one or a class of five thousand. He knew how to adapt lessons for both large and small groups, rich and poor, male and female, educated and uneducated, religious and irreligious, the powerful as well as the disenfranchised. He effectively utilized different learning styles. At times Jesus would lecture as in the Sermon on the Mount, while in other lessons he would ask questions like "Who do you say I am?" (Mt 16:15). He helped students discover embedded concepts and principles when he used real-life scenarios as case studies in his parables. Jesus not only asked questions of his students, he also welcomed questions from his students as well ("Who is my neighbor?" Lk 10:29).

In addition to these methods, Jesus also taught application. His teaching was never limited to just theory, but rather he kept learners interested by providing opportunities for them to apply the theory they had learned. For example, Jesus sent out his disciples with the following instructions:

> As you go, proclaim this message: "The kingdom of heaven has come near." Heal the sick, raise the dead, cleanse those who have leprosy, drive out demons. Freely you have received, freely give.

Do not get any gold or silver or copper to take with you in your belts—no bag for the journey or extra shirt or sandals or a staff. . . . Be as shrewd as snakes and as innocent as doves. (Mt 10:7-10, 16)

Glen T., Ph.D., Comparative Religions, Central Asia

I usually accompany a handful of my students (all converted to Christianity from Islam) on a monthly "servant evangelism" outing. We go to a neighborhood and pick up all the garbage lying around. The neighbors are very curious and immediately ask us what we are doing. Initially they think we are crazy. Our simple response is that we are disciples of Jesus and want to clean the neighborhood in a way similar to the way Jesus wants to clean our hearts.

God usually does very wonderful things at this point. For example, one lady said that as soon as we mentioned "Jesus," all the hair on her arms stood up. We then explained that Jesus was present and his Spirit was touching her. We asked her if we could pray for her and she accepted. This kind of interaction during servant evangelism is common.

We usually clean up for an hour and a half and have six to ten of these kinds of interactions with people. One of the newly converted students has been very faithful in this activity, which has impacted her deeply. All the students who participate give testimony to the presence and power of the Spirit of Jesus. It demonstrates to them that Jesus is alive, he is working, and that his power and presence are real.

Daily they witnessed him living out these principles. They heard his teachings and watched as he healed the sick and raised the dead. As the model teacher, Jesus equipped his students to go and do likewise—to do not only what he said, but what he modeled.

Jesus used a variety of teaching methods that elicited interest and spoke to the culture of the people he was teaching. He used parables, questions, discussion and object lessons. Challenging, enlightening and influencing learners in a dynamic manner made some uneasy, but it allowed them to reevaluate their lives and how they saw the world while giving them important principles to live by.

Christian teachers can draw from these pedagogical techniques in their classrooms. Christian educators teaching overseas must ask, "How do we make our disciplines and our teaching relevant and interesting? How do we provide opportunities for students' application?"

JESUS' RELATIONSHIPS WITH HIS STUDENTS

Jesus as a teacher built relationships with his students. He knew them and called them by name. Teaching Christianly means demonstrating concern for our students. This usually begins by listening to them and being interested in them personally, having their best interests and well-being at heart. Jesus invested in his students' lives by developing mentoring relationships. Mentoring is simply building relationships with your students and being available to them—whether it is playing a game of table tennis or helping edit an academic paper. It is spending time with them, caring about them and giving direction to their lives. Jesus as the model teacher loved his students; Christian teachers must do the same. Following Christ's example as teacher means that students and their learning are central to our teaching strategies.

In order to build these relationships and teach students, Jesus knew and understood his students' needs. He used his knowledge of his learners to meet their individual needs. He was able to stimulate interest and make his lessons relevant because he knew his students and related to them as valuable individuals with worth and dignity. He learned their particular struggles and how they understood the world around them. Teachers must likewise plan and carry out every teaching activity so that students can succeed in their effort to learn.

JESUS' EXPERTISE

When Jesus spoke, people listened. Matthew 7:28-29 shows us the impact of his teaching: "When Jesus had finished saying these things, the crowds were amazed at his teaching, because he taught as one

---

Scott (and Christy) G., J.D., Law Professor, Romania

Every semester we take students out to lunch after class in order to get to know them better. We always pray and ask the Holy Spirit to show us which student to invite on which day.

Iulia lost her dad when she was a little girl. On the anniversary of his death, she was feeling really sad and prayed to God that she would "really like to do something with him [her dad]; have a pizza or something." Christy and I had no idea about this, but guess who we asked out for lunch that day? Yep, it was Iulia. Guess where we went? Yep, we took her out for pizza, and she told us her story. She said she knew she was praying for something impossible, that she couldn't be with her father that day. When we asked her out for pizza, she knew that God had given her us instead.

We have been very close to Iulia ever since. Even though she has been away in France on a scholarship, she communicates regularly via computer. She recently started reading a Bible she borrowed from a fellow student. We had one of our supporters send Iulia her very own Bible from America. We pray that Iulia will believe in Jesus with her life.

---

who had authority." Jesus spoke authoritatively. He had broad knowledge and discerning wisdom and was able to effectively convey and reveal subject matter to students by creating multiple paths to the concepts, principles and ideas he taught. He could clearly communicate the knowledge in a manner that astonished his students.

Following Jesus' model in the classroom means professional preparedness. Jesus spoke from knowledge and truth. "Without full and accurate knowledge of the subject . . . the teacher certainly cannot guide, direct, and test the process of learning" (Gregory, 1884/1982, p. 97). Teaching purposefully, being well-equipped and having knowledge of the field are important parts of following Christ as a teacher. Christians teaching overseas must be able to teach with "clarity, insight and authority" regarding their subjects. They must possess a growing store of knowledge and understanding of their fields and of teaching in order to emulate Jesus. They must grasp how their subject area is organized, linked to other disciplines and applied to real-world settings. Professional preparedness is crucial in the practical application of living out a Christian witness.

JESUS AS A SERVANT

Jesus was a servant. He came to serve, not to be served. As Christian educators serving in secular classrooms overseas, we are called to represent Christ's hands and feet. That means serving others.

What is involved in serving? Being a servant means we are humble. Humility is demonstrated to students and colleagues through a spirit and actions of servanthood, gentleness and meekness. Taking on the spirit of a servant is vital to reflect Christ in one's teaching (McCarthy, 2001).

One way Jesus demonstrated to his students that he was a servant was by washing their feet. Foot washing in ancient Israel was a job for a slave. No self-respecting nonslave would ever wash another's feet. For a rabbi—a teacher—to wash his students' feet was unheard of. Yet Jesus did this for his students as a way of modeling for them humility, brokenness and unconditional love. As Christian educators serving overseas, we must ask, "What does it mean for me to wash my students' feet and my colleagues' feet?" This will look different for each person, but the principle of servanthood remains the same. We are to serve our students with humility and unconditional love. We are to demonstrate to them that, like Christ, we are willing to lay down our lives for them. We are willing to live sacrificially for them. We are willing to do everything we can to help meet their educational, spiritual and emotional needs. This may mean working hard to grade papers carefully and clearly. It may mean going beyond the job description and helping a student fill out an application for a university abroad. It may mean doing menial tasks such as cleaning our

Bill M., Ph.D., Political Science, Prague

My student Gabor broke his leg slipping on ice on his way to meet with me for coffee. We had scheduled a time together at a local café to discuss his thoughts on C. S. Lewis's *Mere Christianity*. I received a call from him telling me he had fallen down a very steep hill taking a shortcut to the tram stop. He was injured badly. I went out and found him in great pain, perhaps close to shock. It was very cold that day. His knee was swelling terribly. After a very slow process of carrying him down the hill, I drove him to the emergency room. He hadn't had anything to eat or drink all day so I got him something while we waited to see the doctor. After x-rays and an examination by the doctor, it was determined that his femur was broken right at the knee. They decided to do surgery right away. So I left the hospital to pick up a few items for him.

When I returned, Gabor had not yet had surgery. I brought him a change of clothes, some cash and some food (in Czech hospitals, you aren't provided with meals or even fluids; you have to provide all that for yourself or someone has to provide for you). He was thrilled to see me and said that when the door was opening he was hoping that it was his mom. Well, I'm not his mom, but I provided him with access to my phone (his had run out of power) so that he could call his mom. He was very thankful to talk to her.

Later Gabor was picked up by his parents to recover at home in Slovakia. He should be back in Prague soon again and plans to contact me then. I pray for Gabor, for healing and for this event to be an opportunity for God to speak into his life and that I would be a witness to him during this time. We did talk briefly about Lewis. Gabor, it appears, is still very much on the fence, avoiding the choice that lies before him! But as always, we are trusting God.

classrooms, emptying trashcans and straightening desks—all without complaint. Whatever it requires, we must deliberately live out Christ's servant attitude and with a spirit of humility serve our students as unto Christ.

Jesus as servant met the needs of individuals—he fed them, he healed them and he taught them principles that would forever change their lives. Jesus also rebuked them when necessary, but because of his great love for them he rebuked them perfectly and without defeating their enthusiasm or their passion. All of these are ways in which we can follow Jesus' example of serving our students in an overseas classroom.

JESUS PRAYED FOR HIS STUDENTS

Jesus prayed for his students. He prayed for their unity, their protection from the evil one, their safety, their future, and that God would sanctify them (Jn 17:6-19). Jesus prayed for his students' eyes and ears to be opened. We must do the same. Praying for students is a vital part of building relationships with them and serving them. It is also a powerful tool in learning to love students. Never underestimate the power of prayer.

Many classes taught by Christians overseas are in countries where Christian ministry or traditional missionary work is not permitted. Most students in these creative-access countries do not have anyone in the world interceding for them before God. In Muslim, Hindu, Buddhist, secular, communist or atheistic societies, there may be no viable Christian witness anywhere in those students' lives. Kneeling with a class roster and praying for each student by name every day is one of the most significant ways that a Christian educator can follow Jesus' example as teacher.

Praying is also a vital part of lesson preparation. Pray over your lesson plans. As we follow Christ's example and strive to honor him in the classroom, we must recognize our teaching as a holy calling and sacred work. When we enter our classroom, we must be deliberate in bringing Christ with us. As we bring his presence into that room, it becomes a sanctuary for worship of the living God. Even if our students are not aware of it, when we who love God cry out for him to be honored in our teaching, we are actively engaged in an act of worship. The classroom becomes a sacred place where we ask for the Holy Spirit's anointing as we present our lesson to our students. With our hearts and minds focused on Christ our teaching becomes a sacred act.

JESUS LIVED WHAT HE TAUGHT

Role modeling and "walking the walk" are what we mean by "teaching good." A role model is an individual who is unusually effective in inspiring others not from just the spoken word but through behavior. Modeling Christian values and behavior is sometimes very attractive to students overseas because it may be different from what they are accustomed to seeing. When students witness firsthand the fruit of the spirit (love, joy, peace, patience, kindness, goodness, faithfulness, gentleness and self-control), they will probably wonder why you behave as you do.

Students respond to a teacher's role modeling. For example, when teachers show a high interest and enthusiasm and seek relevance for the subject matter, there is a chance that students will gain interest in what they are studying. By modeling critical thinking and questioning, students develop critical thinking skills and learn how to process the world around them. Teachers need to determine the behaviors that they want their students to display (teaching good) and then examine their own pedagogy to see if these behaviors are being modeled inside and outside their classroom (teaching well).

You can't "teach good" if you don't "teach well." Poor teaching does not normally change lives. You can't teach life-changing principles to your students if you don't teach well. A Christian teacher may sacrifice many things to teach overseas and may endure difficult living conditions in order to teach good things to students, but if the teacher is a poor teacher, she will be ineffective. Mary's teaching pointed Maria to Christ because Mary's teaching was well-planned, she was genuinely concerned about her students' learning and she kept a good attitude even in the midst of harsh living conditions. As a result Mary was able to teach the *ultimate* good.

Christ taught compassion, and his students saw that he was compassionate to others, especially the marginalized and despised of society. Jesus taught about loving one's neighbor, and his students learned a new definition of neighbor through the story of the Good Samaritan. Living out what you teach requires careful examination of your teaching and lifestyle. It requires consistency of behavior. Much human learning occurs while watching others. Students watch foreign teachers and consciously or unconsciously store behavior in their memories. Later these ideas become models for their own vocations, relationships and behavior.

Jesus was comfortable with people from all walks of life. He had an authentic concern and love for others. He genuinely reached out to people without regard for where they were from or what they did for a living. Part of teaching well is acknowledging the significance of every human being with whom you come in contact. As C. S. Lewis (1949/1996) declared, there are no "ordinary people. You have never talked to a mere mortal" (p. 39). Human beings made in the image of God are valuable, and part of following Jesus' example as teacher is treating people both inside and outside the classroom with respect.

APPLYING JESUS' METHODS IN DISTANT CLASSROOMS

By comparing and contrasting the way Jesus taught with those of culturally responsive teachers, we can gain insight into better ways to serve in a distant classroom. Villegas and Lucas (2002) identify six characteristics of teachers who are responsive to cultural differences and offer effective teaching and learning in a crosscultural classroom. The chart on pages 104 and 105 illustrates the characteristics of culturally responsive teaching and compares them to what we know about Jesus' teaching.

So what does culturally responsive teaching mean for us as Christian teachers in distant classrooms? It means cultivating a desire and willingness to engage those who are different. This is not a superficial relationship but rather requires hard work to gain an understanding of the culture and grasp how culture influences teaching and learning.

Christians who teach overseas have a life-changing platform of eternal significance. They have the opportunity to live out these life-changing principles before students both inside and outside the classroom. We have no better educational model to follow than the master teacher—Jesus Christ himself, who always practiced what he preached and taught. In this chapter we have seen how Christ made a difference in students' lives with his teaching, mentoring and role-modeling. Based on this framework, the next chapter will show more specifically how Christ's example can be applied in practical ways in the overseas classroom.

Roberta G., Ph.D., Biology, Asia

KE is in my Scientific Writing class. She stayed after class the first day and asked me if I was a Christian. She had met other foreigner Christians and had a feeling I was also one. She seemed intrigued that a biologist could be a person of faith. I could sense God was working in her heart and began praying for opportunities to share his love with her. I invited her to come and watch movies at my apartment. (Every Friday night I show Christian films for any students that want to come.) She came and stayed after the movie to talk with me.

KE recently told me that she had decided to believe in God. I encouraged her to come to the Wednesday night Bible study I hold in my home. She began coming and asked great questions like "Why did Jesus need to die?" It is so incredible to see God drawing KE to himself and to have the privilege of being part of that process. I gave her a parallel Bible (her language and English), and she is reading it. I pray that very soon she will accept Jesus.

GOING DEEPER, GOING FURTHER

Questions to Consider

1. What are some practical ways you can be a servant to students, colleagues and other host nationals?

2. What are possible personal issues that might prevent you from serving others?

Table 5 (Adapted from Villegas & Lucas, 2002.)

Culturally Responsive Teachers	Jesus' Teaching
Culturally responsive teachers recognize that different worldviews, social interactions and approaches to learning are deeply influenced by factors such as race/ethnicity, gender, social class, language and nationality. This understanding enables teachers to cross the cultural boundaries that separate them from their students.	Jesus understood his students. He knew their weaknesses and their strengths. He spoke differently to Peter the fisherman ("Come, follow me, . . . and I will send you out to fish for people," Mt 4:19) than he did to Matthew the tax collector ("Follow me . . . for I have not come to call the righteous, but sinners," Mt 9:9, 13).
Culturally responsive teachers affirm student views from diverse backgrounds, seeing learning resources in all students rather than viewing differences as problems.	Jesus affirmed his students; he listened to their different perspectives. But he critically challenged inaccuracy in the light of truth. James and John wanted prominence when Jesus began his rule: "Let one of us sit at your right and the other at your left." Jesus said, "You don't know what you are asking" (Mk 10:36-38). He then used that situation to teach all his disciples a lesson about leaders being servants and the first being last.
Culturally responsive teachers believe they have a duty and a responsibility to bring about changes that will make education better for students. They know how to challenge errors in the system, but they also know how to challenge students' thinking with the truth.	Jesus revolutionized students' thinking about all of life. He told them it was easier for a camel to go through the eye of a needle than for a rich person to enter the kingdom of God (Mt 19:24). They were shocked. They had never heard teaching like this before. They asked, "Who then can be saved?" because they believed wealth was a sign of God's favor; if a rich man couldn't get into heaven, then who could? Jesus motivated students to see the world differently. His teaching was life transforming as well as relevant.

Culturally Responsive Teachers	Jesus' Teaching
Culturally responsive teachers are familiar with their students' prior knowledge and beliefs. They know that these are derived from both students' personal and cultural experiences.	Jesus had great insight into his students' lives. He made learning a part of their lives. He connected an action with their prior knowledge and by this reinforced the lesson. Jesus said to his students, "You have heard" (Mt 5) and then built his lesson on what they had been taught (i.e., prior knowledge).
Culturally responsive teachers see learning as an active process in which the learner is bringing something of value to the table: new information, ideas, principles and other stimuli. They see teaching as participatory.	Jesus' teaching was student-centered. He stimulated thought, guided learning, and challenged his students to consider and apply new ways of thinking. In the feeding of the crowds, Jesus said to his students, "You give them something to eat" (Lk 9:13). And they participated in the miracle, which was in reality a life-application lesson: God provides.
Culturally responsive teachers design instruction that builds on what students already know while at the same time stretching them beyond the familiar.	To elicit what his students believed, Jesus asked probing questions: "Who do you say I am?" (asked of Peter in Mt 16:15). He made comparisons of what the students knew: "This is what the kingdom of God is like" (Mk 4:26). He used what they understood to help them comprehend his radically new lesson/message. Jesus challenged the familiar. His teachings centered on presenting truth and allowing it to crash in on students' worldviews and presuppositions.

3. What are some issues or situations that might prevent you from being a role model for Christ? What will you do to prevent or address these?

4. For example, you might struggle being patient waiting in crowds when there is no queuing up in that nation. What will you do to prevent losing patience and thus hurting your witness?

Suggested Reading List

Books

Jesus the Master Teacher, Herman H. Harrell. Written in 1920 but is a great read. (Available online at: http://books.google.com/books)

Rock Solid Teacher: Discover the Joy of Teaching Like Jesus, Greg Carlson

Teaching Like Jesus, LaVerne Tolbert

Teaching That Works: Strategies From Scripture for Classrooms Today, Cliff Schimmels

Articles

These two articles are good resources for finding culturally appropriate illustrations and examples:

Darrell Whiteman, "Effective Communication of the Gospel Amid Cultural Diversity" *Missiology* vol. 12, no. 3 (1982) (http://www.asmweb.org/missiology.htm)

David Hesselgrave, "The Role of Culture in Communication," *Perspectives on the World Christian Movement: A Reader* (3rd edition)

REFERENCE LIST

Friedeman, M. (1990). *The master plan of teaching: Understanding and applying the teaching styles of Jesus*. Wheaton, IL: Victor Books.

Gregory, J. M. (1982). *The seven laws of teaching* (Rev. ed.). Grand Rapids: Baker. (Original work published 1884).

Lewis, C. S. (1996). *The weight of glory* (5th ed.). New York: Touchstone. (Original work published 1949).

McCarthy, T. (2001). Living with Christian integrity in a global context. *Discernment*, 8(1), 8-9.

Villegas, A. M., & Lucas, T. (2002). *Educating culturally responsive teachers: A coherent approach*. New York: SUNY.

6

Nuts and Bolts

Practical Applications for Effective Teaching in Overseas Classrooms

O Captain! My Captain! rise up and hear the bells;

Rise up—for you the flag is flung—for you the bugle trills;

For you bouquets and ribbon'd wreaths—for you the shores a-crowding;

For you they call, the swaying mass, their eager faces turning.

WALT WHITMAN

D r. Cliff Schimmels[1] took a year off from his university in the United States, and he and his wife went to teach in China. There Cliff taught

---

[1] Cliff Schimmels authored over thirty books on topics ranging from education to child rearing. He was a passionate and extraordinary educator who had a tremendous impact on students and colleagues around the world. Cliff was a full professor of education at both Wheaton College and Lee University. As the story in this chapter illustrates, he was an excellent border crosser. Cliff died in 2001. The practical applications in this chapter are based on an unpublished manual called "Cliff's Notes" that Cliff wrote for new teachers.

English and graduate education and held faculty development workshops. Cliff helped whenever he could by doing whatever he was asked.

He taught Walt Whitman's poem "O Captain! My Captain!" to his undergraduate English classes. Cliff worked hard to help his Chinese students grasp the concepts of Whitman's words but was never quite sure if the students actually caught on to the deeper meaning of the poem. Were they actually getting it? Cliff was always thinking of ways to help his students learn, and part of his teaching strategy was to participate in his students' lives. He went to their soccer games, watched them run track, attended concerts with them and had most of them in his home at one time or another throughout the year.

To say Cliff was a good teacher is not quite accurate. Cliff was a great teacher. He was always prepared for class. He never flew by the seat of his pants, and he saw the classroom as sacred, his place of ministry. Cliff knew his subject matter well. He was an expert in his field, and he loved teaching. It is no exaggeration to say that Cliff Schimmels impacted thousands of lives, both students and faculty, at home and abroad.

After serving a year in China, Cliff and his wife packed up their belongings one hot and humid summer morning and started the long journey back home. Because they had to catch a flight in Shanghai—six hours away by train—they rose before four o'clock that morning and quietly left their small apartment, trying not to wake their neighbors. As they left, they heard a commotion on a small hill just under the street lights. The gray, misty dawn revealed hundreds of students with bouquets of flowers, ribboned wreaths and red flags. Six young men in the very front of the crowd were holding a large white banner with red lettering: "O Captain! My Captain!" It was then that Cliff realized they had indeed gotten it.

How could anyone so deeply impact the lives of his students? What must teachers do to have such an influence? What can I do while teaching in an overseas classroom to engage students at such a personal level?

This type of teacher is rare. Honestly, not many of us will ever have a farewell like Cliff's. But we all *can* and *will* have some degree of impact on our students. More importantly, effective and influential teachers use some basic nuts and bolts of teaching that enable them to inspire and impact their students' lives.

Duane Elmer cites a study (2000) that Canadians Hawes and Kealey conducted on effectiveness in overseas assignments around the globe. They defined *effectiveness* as satisfactory personal adjustment, positive interpersonal relationships with host nationals and task accomplishment (p. 1). The study showed that *professional competency*—being trained to do the job and do it well—aided tremendously in ministry effectiveness.

In this chapter we will prepare you to do your job well by giving you practical approaches, strategies and helpful hints that will aid your teaching in distant classrooms. This is the "how to" of teaching well in a different culture. Objectives, teaching methods and organizing class presentations are vital for teaching. But our integrity—*who we are*—as teachers influences students even more than our lectures. Cliff Schimmels's "O Captain" experience demonstrates the impact one teacher can have on an entire campus.

It wasn't just Cliff's personality; it was his practice that made the difference. Not only do students learn from our pedagogy, they also learn lessons from the comments we make and the materials we use. Students learn from the way we treat them both in and out of the classroom. These lessons can be positive or negative.

As you read this chapter, think about the teachers who most influenced your life. What characteristics did they have that motivated you? What did they do that influenced you? More importantly, how can their example be adapted to your particular crosscultural setting? Let's consider some of the basics of teaching well and see how good teachers' identity and integrity can make a difference in the lives of their students.

ANALYZING THE CHALLENGE

Doing a good job means knowing your students and understanding the educational system that brought you to them. If possible, do research about your host culture and its students *before* moving there. Find out what approach to education the government or ministry of education uses (see UNESCO's website at http://www.unesco.org). Do they use teacher-centered or student-centered approaches to learning? Discover their learning styles (see appendix C for Gardner's Multiple Intelligences Theory) and use this information to plan lessons and assessments. You will need to adapt these ideas for your particular situation. The following applications are our variations of "Cliff's Notes." Remember that these are ideas and suggestions that you will need to adjust to meet your own classroom situation, cultural issues, student age group and teaching style.

PRACTICAL APPLICATIONS FOR TEACHING

Before Class

1. Choose your clothing wisely. *Do not* be a distraction to your students. Don't overdress so they think you are vain, but don't look unprofessional either. Try not to be a distraction by your clothing or hairstyle. Think about your former professors. Certainly you remember at least one whose appearance was so odd it mesmerized you and you couldn't hear the lecture. Dress appropriately for the culture (some universities do not permit faculty to wear jeans). Find out what your colleagues wear and try to fit in.

2. Plan from your teaching objective. And you better have an objective! Never walk into a classroom to teach without a lesson plan. Write down your goals and objectives for that class and make certain they are in line with your overall class syllabus. Use this as a compass and you will stay on course. (See appendix A for a lesson plan template.)

3. Learn your students' names. The most effective tool for effective teaching in the classroom is learning each of your students' names. Make a seating chart, call roll every day, make

nametags, take digital pictures of each student and mark them with their names. It doesn't matter how you do it—but you need to do it. Also pray for them every day; praying over your roster helps you learn their names. Note: Photographs may be forbidden in some Muslim nations. Check on appropriateness in your host culture.

4. Arrange the furniture in a way that is conducive to your objective. If you want to have discussion groups, you'll need to make sure the desks can be moved. In many countries, desks and chairs are bolted down. If that is the case in your classroom, get permission to unbolt them. Find ways to make the classroom a great place for learning. If you want to use chairs and nothing else, do it. Take command of that classroom, but know why you are moving the furniture. Prepare students for the change and make sure your purpose matches your objective. Also, make sure you provide colleagues with a sound and well-thought-out educational argument to justify your "different" approach to teaching.

5. Put up bulletin boards or posters that relate to your topic/theme. Let those things reinforce your subject matter. For example, use an Occupational Safety and Health Administration (www.osha .gov) bulletin for business management classes; display movie posters for English classes (be culturally sensitive about these and issues of modesty, etc.); or use pictures of your favorite historical figures if you are teaching history. When students are learning subject matter in a language not their own, truly *a picture paints a thousand words.* Sometimes your bulletin

> `Objective:` a statement that describes skills, abilities, or content knowledge that a student will learn from your class. Objectives generally relate to goals or aims within a lesson plan.

boards and posters may have to be mobile if your classroom changes often. In some countries there is a high likelihood of theft of anything left in the classroom. Find out what will work and adjust accordingly.

6. Write your objectives on the board. Every day assure your students that you know where you are taking them. They look to you as their guide. Write it on the board, for your sake and for theirs. For example, "Today's lesson objective is to calculate new ways of measuring moisture in wheat." Or "Today's lesson objective is to write paragraphs that describe."

7. Post your rules! If you don't want chewing gum in your class, say so. If you do not allow drinks, smoking or spitting (seriously, this is a big problem in some countries); if you want cell phones turned off; or if you don't want languages other than English spoken in your classroom, make a poster that lists your rules and put that in your classroom. This is part of letting students know your expectations and can be used as teachable moments by explaining the reasoning and thoughts behind these rules. At times you will have a few students who lack an understanding of appropriate classroom behavior and this can seriously disrupt the learning environment. Classroom management is always a difficult issue. While Teri taught overseas, she found it helpful to construct a poster that stated what she termed "The Five Big Rules." She used this for two reasons: (1) it gave her something to point out to students so she did not have to keep repeating the rules; and (2) students have no excuses like "I forgot" or "I don't remember you saying that." At times, the national teachers wanted her to keep the poster in shared classrooms so they could use it with their students. A nice influence on colleagues, this is one strategy for classroom management that worked well. Keep in mind that you will need to adapt this idea to your classroom, focusing on the level you are teaching and your teaching style. The key is to develop and enforce important rules for appropriate classroom behavior so that

the most important thing occurs—students learn.

8. Put a daily quotation on the board. Sometimes you can explain it, but you don't always have to. Sometimes you can just let them ponder it. Your students will come to love this quote of the day the way many Americans enjoy David Letterman's top-ten lists. Use the quotes for a purpose if you like. Use quotes that support or enhance your lesson, and don't be afraid to let those quotes reflect your worldview. When the host nation allows, use Bible verses with the citation. If you are in a nation where that is not appropriate, you don't always have to write the source of the quote. For example, "A merry heart does good like a medicine" (an ancient proverb).

9. Do your own assignment. Make sure it is doable in your host culture (do they have the resources to research a twenty-page paper?). Make sure it really reinforces your lecture or the principle you are covering. Don't blindly assign things without knowing the purpose behind the exercise. Do not give students busywork.

Class Begins

1. Greet students at the door every time class starts, when they come in (which means you have to be there early). Relate to your students as individuals. Acknowledge their existence and their significance. Ask how their day is going or ask about family members. Take an interest in each one. No matter the age of your students, this is vitally important and shows them that you care and that they matter.

2. Start on time—if at all possible. You are modeling behavior you want your students to duplicate. By starting class when it is scheduled to start, you show them you value their time and that the subject matter is important to you. But remember the concept of "on time" varies among cultures. Discuss with students your beliefs about time and theirs. Try to come to an agreement regarding the start of class. Mike, for example, because of the frustrations of trying to get students to class on time in his Middle Eastern uni-

versity, decided to start class fifteen minutes later than officially scheduled. Then he used the extra time to meet with students who arrived on schedule. They discussed class concerns or he helped them with their assignments. This really solved the problem in a productive way, because students started then arriving thirty to forty-five minutes *before* the scheduled time just to talk with him and get the extra help. As a result, fewer and fewer students came late to class.

3. On the first day of class don't assume your students know each other. Have them introduce themselves. Often when we are strangers in a strange land we assume that everyone else around us is somehow acquainted. That is not the case. If possible, on the first day of class put them in groups and have them interview each other (or someone they do not know). Have them introduce themselves and tell three things about themselves: for example, their favorite food, their favorite novel and their favorite subject in school. Start building a community within that classroom and they will respond better to you *and* to each other. Caution: make sure questions are culturally appropriate and gender issues are considered when pairing students up.

4. Use a starter. Some educators call this the "introduction." It's a brief activity or event at the beginning of the lesson that engages students' attention and focuses their thoughts on class. It is a tool you use to get their attention and set the tone. It has two objectives:

• To help students make the mental, emotional and physical transition from where they are to where they need to be in your class.

• To introduce the lesson for the day and stimulate some kind of interest in your topic and objective.

    Examples: A relevant story, open-ended questions, a quote relevant to the lesson, a recent news item in the paper or on TV, a brain teaser or a riddle.

During Class

1. Move around some. Don't get in the habit of standing behind the lectern or desk—even if that is the standard practice at your school. Keep in mind cultural issues such as students accustomed to professors standing behind the lectern. Slowly introduce students to your "philosophy" of the teacher moving in the classroom. Warn students you are trying something new and then move around the classroom. Guard against pacing and don't jingle change in your pockets.

2. If you write on the blackboard, don't stand in the way. Sometimes teaching well is just a matter of common sense and practical thinking. Keep in mind that your students are human beings. You as the teacher must try to anticipate what they need, like the ability to see what you have on the board. If you write on the chalkboard, move out of the way and allow them plenty of time to see what you've written. Also, for those who can utilize technology, try not to stand in front of the projector when you are showing PowerPoint slides.

3. Have a "purpose-driven" chalkboard (or PowerPoint). Students tend to believe that anything written on that chalkboard or highlighted in a PowerPoint presentation is important. Use that to your advantage. Give them plenty of time to write it all down before you erase it or go to the next slide. Usually you will give a written exam from whatever you have written on the board, so keep track of your notes. Use these tools wisely because most students believe that what you write on your chalkboard is more important than what you say.

4. Anticipate confrontation and conflict and prepare well for it. When Teri taught in China, there was a student in her class whose father was a powerful leader in the province. This student constantly disrupted class, talked on his cell phone and made inappropriate comments—an unusual situation in China where students nor-

mally respect their university instructors. Teri understood Chinese culture enough to know that she should not cause this young man to lose face in front of his classmates. She also knew about the political situation and that making this student angry could cause more problems for her since his father was a leader.

Teri prayed and asked God to give her wisdom to handle this student. After praying and thinking about the cultural context, she devised a plan. She calculated how much the university paid her per class, and she put that amount of money in an envelope. The next class, she gave the envelope to the disruptive student and said to the class, "Mr. Wang is better equipped than I to teach this class. I am paying him my wages to take the responsibility of teaching all of you English." And she went home. She knew that Chinese culture worked best when pressure came from the group and not from a one-on-one confrontation. She also knew that disciplining this student was not an option; kicking him out of class wouldn't work.

In less than an hour a student representative was knocking on her apartment door asking her to please come back to class, assuring her that Mr. Wang would not be a problem any longer. And he wasn't. Students needed the class to graduate, so they pressured their classmate to stop disrupting.

5. Let your students plan your lesson—be in tune with their needs and, as much as possible, their wants. This may mean you change some course objectives and let go of some of your pet projects if they do not meet your students' needs. For example, one young, inexperienced English teacher planned to teach her students how to order at a restaurant using an English-language menu. She had used this lesson with ESL[2] students in the U.S. and it worked very

---

[2]English as a second language (ESL) refers to English taught to non-native speakers in an English-speaking country, usually in a bilingual setting. For example, English taught to immigrant communities in North America for whom English is not their mother tongue. English as a foreign language (EFL) refers to English language taught in non-English-speaking countries.

well. What she didn't realize was that none of her new students would ever leave their country, much less use an English-language menu. The lesson wasn't appropriate for her students, no matter how well it worked back home.

6. Answer the Six Big Questions: who, what, when, where, why and how. Teaching is communicating, and good communication requires you answer as many of the Big Questions as possible. Think about these questions as you prepare your lesson plans and class activities.

   - Why is this material important?

   - Who are the movers and shakers behind this principle/idea or event?

   - What are the lessons we can draw from this? What are the applications we can make?

   - When do we use it? When did it happen? When did it change?

   - Where is it most used? Where did it occur? Where did it originate?

   - How does it impact lives?

   Clearly explain new concepts and principles when introducing new ideas. This requires the instructor to answer as many of the Big Questions as possible.

7. Teach in intervals. You can use simple intervals like beginning, middle and end. Studies show that most adults have an attention span of about fifteen minutes, so break your lesson plan up into several activities, such as lecture, group discussion, student presentations and review—that's about an hour's worth of material.

8. Do you feel like you're talking to a wall? Check to see if they heard you. Ask specific questions to specific students: "Karl, what is the first principle for starting your own business?" If they

come from a culture that is not accustomed to answering questions, teach them how to ask and answer questions. Ease them into the process at first by having them write questions on slips of paper. Give them the tools they need to succeed in your class.

9. Show them the idea. Don't just tell them. Think about your class ahead of time. Think about all the terms you will use both in your objective and in the carrying out of that objective. Then plan techniques that will help your students see the idea. Remember: A picture paints a thousand words. Use case studies and lots of illustrations and examples. Use the concrete to help explain the abstract. For example, in a science lecture about the pros and cons of cloning, don't just say cloning has drawbacks. Show them: "I think cloning has drawbacks. The weaknesses of the donor will be passed on to the clone. If you clone an entire army of Arnold Schwarzeneggers, then all your enemy has to do is find his Achilles' heel and destroy your entire army. Diversity is good—in sheep, cattle and in human beings." An illustration they can relate to and grasp helps them understand the underlying abstract theories behind the principle.

10. Teach listening. Know the difference between hearing and listening; help your students understand the difference as well. Hearing is the physical reception of the voice, whereas listening is the mental processing of the received message. Make sure your students know how to listen and not just hear.

11. Search for the missing concept. Find out what your students are not grasping and reconstruct your approach. Have more than one way to present an idea. Don't become frustrated if they do not understand it on the first try.

12. Use groups when appropriate. This is known in education as *collaborative learning*. Studies have shown that Jean Piaget (1896-1980) was right. Some people do learn better in community. Groups provide an environment that can richly enhance the

learning process. Cooperative learning develops students' social skills, raises the self-esteem of students, raises student achievement, challenges able students to help less able students, and helps meet the overall goal of student success (Slavin, 1990; Cruickshank et al., 1999). Furthermore, small groups in the classroom can create safe environments for students to take chances and express new ideas. Students build community

> *Collaborative learning (also known as cooperative learning):* an interactive approach to teamwork that enables students, paired or in small groups, to combine their individual skills and resources to find creative solutions, perform tasks or design projects.

within the classroom by having groups solve problems, practice language, critique works of art or literature, or create projects like getting a politician into office. Groups provide a more realistic social context for learning. (For more information on collaborative learning experiences, go to http://teaching.berkeley.edu/bgd/collaborative.html.)

13. Show them the big picture: "You'll need this someday because . . ." or "This is important to know when . . ." This provides motivation and clarity and helps students want to learn because they can link this lesson to real life.

14. Let them think. Create strategies that give them the opportunity to use their thinking skills when dealing with your subject matter. Use simulations and writing assignments. Use questions and brainstorming. Come up with exercises that will build their creative thinking and problem-solving skills. An example for an ethics class: "So Yuri, what would you do if your wife was dying and you needed medicine you couldn't afford? Would you steal to

save a human life?" Get them thinking about the principle or concept you're teaching.

15. Develop questioning skills. Learn to teach with the Socratic method of questions and dialogue (see suggested websites at the end of this chapter). Prepare your students to use it. When you ask questions, their answers help them synthesize the concepts and summarize the material.

16. Respect their vulnerability. The process of learning is a humbling experience. Don't embarrass your students in front of the entire class. Build trust so that they can learn more effectively. Let them know they are in a safe place to learn, to develop and even to make mistakes.

17. Give reading assignments, and make sure *you* read them! Know what you are assigning. Be familiar with the text and the materials. If you are caught off guard, it can make students feel you are either unprepared or not knowledgeable. Worse, it may make them feel like you don't care, they don't matter and the material isn't important.

18. Share what you *personally* are reading. Let students in on what

---

Bill W., J.D., Law Professor, Asia

Monica, a student from my first Moot Court Team, became a good friend to me and my wife. She became a regular attendee of our weekly book club meeting. This Easter, after a lot of study, prayer, consideration and "counting the cost," Monica told us she wanted to become a Christian. We celebrated the resurrection of Jesus Christ on Easter morning by rejoicing together with Monica and two other new believers and sharing Communion. It was one of the best Easter mornings we have ever experienced!

you like to read and what you are currently reading. It doesn't matter if you are teaching business, agriculture or English. Allowing students to see your appreciation for reading not only gives them some insight into you, but may give them a greater interest for reading as well.

19. Use writing to help them remember. Plan assigned writing exercises that will have them repeat and recall what was taught in class. Use writing as a tool for reflection on a principle or concept you introduced in the lesson.

20. Teach test taking. Some of your students may have never been given open-ended or essay questions in their entire academic careers. Don't spring it on them, but prepare them for it. Explain to them what you are looking for in each type of test question.

21. Speak with confidence. This confidence needs to come from your thorough preparation; it shouldn't be just an act. In some cultures it is inappropriate for the teacher to say, "I don't know." If asked a question that you don't know the answer to, respond this way: "Great question. I want to give that question a full and meaningful answer. Let's not take time out today, but let's address it first thing tomorrow in depth." Then go home and study like crazy to find the answer. This is especially important for young teachers. Not all cultures appreciate transparency and will see your "I don't know" response as a lack of knowledge, as a weakness. You can lose your credibility for the entire year. So, be wise and careful and try to postpone questions you don't know the answer to until you find the answer.

22. Build dreams. Do you remember a favorite teacher who inspired you to do something? who told you that you would make a great leader, or were a talented artist? Model that behavior. Help students see their potential. Be specific. For example, "Juan Carlos, that presentation today was excellent. Have you ever thought about becoming a teacher?"

23. Learn to hear the applause. When a student gives you a genuine compliment, receive it and let it soak in. When students perform well, grasp a concept or learn new approaches to the subject matter, consider it all applause and a positive reflection on your teaching. Take time to enjoy it.

24. Leave time for closure. Review the class content for that day: ask someone to summarize, link it to previous lessons and show the important role it plays in their overall learning. Do a three-minute "write down" by asking the students to write down:

    1. One concept they learned.

    2. One concept they did not understand.

    3. One thing about the lesson they already knew.

    Then use those points to help in planning your next lesson.

After Class

1. Tell your students goodbye as they leave. These students are important because they are *your* students. They are the leaders of tomorrow who have listened and learned from you. Encourage, smile, and remind them of assignments, activities or a movie night at your house. Let them know you like them and that you are glad they are in your class. One Romanian university student told her American professor, "You are the first professor in my life that has ever called me by name."

2. Don't take things personally. Students are at a difficult stage and often struggle with roommates, relationships, romance issues and a host of other anxieties. They can be moody. It's not about you, so don't take it personally.

3. Clean your own classroom and take out the trash. Keep your classroom clean and decent. It will speak volumes to your students and colleagues. Your classroom is a holy place—the sanctuary where you worship God with your preparedness, your love for your stu-

dents, and your desire, whether openly expressed or not, to bring glory to God. Model for students respect for your classroom and they will develop that respect as well. Your love for your students is shown by your personal willingness to do the menial task of cleaning the room.

4. Read their papers and grade their work. Get their graded assignments back to them in a timely fashion. You asked them to turn in assignments by a deadline, now you return them in the same way. Reading and responding to what they have taken time to write illustrates to them not only the importance of the assignment, but their own importance as well. When you return the assignments at the time you promised, you show respect for your students. View grading as a teaching opportunity by asking questions and writing quality comments on students' papers that get them to think.

5. Test for your objectives. Don't throw your students a curve ball. A good rule of thumb is that if more than 70 percent of the class got a test question wrong, then chances are it was a bad question. Throw it out. Take it out of the test score. A side benefit of this is it lets students see you are fair and just—perhaps some of them have never seen this in an instructor.

6. Be prepared for parent involvement. This is tricky at the college level. But be aware that many cultures around the world are more familial than North America. In places like Latin America, Russia, Ukraine and Afghanistan, many parents want to be a part of their children's education. Unlike in North America, the majority of college students around the world do not leave home to go to school; they attend the university in their own city. As a result, parents are close at hand and sometimes they like to be very involved in their children's education. You might find they'll ask you to change a child's grade, excuse a long absence and even to allow their child to enroll in an already filled class. Just be prepared.

7. Watch them do their thing! Show up for concerts where they are

John C., Ph.D., Christian Studies, Lithuania

I was in quite a hurry when Valeriya and her mother came to my office before the start of the new semester. I had to rush off to a meeting and I wondered what could possibly be so urgent that they would both visit me here between semesters. Valeriya had done well in my Introduction to the Bible class, where we went step-by-step through the story of the Old Testament. All of my students knew that we would be taking up the New Testament in the spring. Why were she and her mother in my office?

She told me that she was having difficulty enrolling in my section for the second half of the Bible course. She had brought her mother with her to see the registrar in hopes of resolving the issue. I explained to her that both of my sections were full and indeed had a lengthy waiting list. But I assured her that I would see what I could do to get her on the roll. It was then that she looked into my face and implored, "You don't understand. I must take your class . . . I have to hear the rest of the story!"

For Valeriya the issue was not just one of getting the right course schedule. She had become enthralled by the story of God's redemptive work toward his creation. And now it was imperative to her that she hear the "rest of the story." God's story.

Valeriya and seventy-five other students are now hearing the rest of the story. Three days a week we encounter the New Testament in my Introduction to the Bible classes. For most of my students, this academic year is the first they have heard of God's love for his creation, and more personally, for them. God is working in ways beyond our dreams. Some days I still cannot believe that we are here and that God would choose to use us in such a way.

performing, go to sporting events and plays, see their artwork at local exhibits. Participate in your students' lives. Be their biggest fan.

8. Don't talk about students with other students or even with colleagues. Don't discuss their issues at school. Honor them and they will honor you.

GOING DEEPER, GOING FURTHER

Exercise/Activity

Consider several of the following teaching strategies that you might use in your teaching. Identify if the strategy is more teacher- or student-centered and why? How might you adapt the teacher-centered strategies so they contain more active learning? How might these strategies be more or less effective considering the cultural factors in the country you are teaching?

Brainstorming	Interactive media
Cooperative learning	Journal writing
Debate	Library research
Demonstration	Panel discussion
Discovery	project
Question and answer	Simulation
Field trip	Review and practice
Guest presenter	Role Play
Assignments	Reading
Individualized instruction	Study guide

Suggested Readings

Effective Instruction, Tamar Levin and Ruth Long (secular)

A Handbook for Adjunct/Part-Time Faculty and Teachers of Adults (4th edition), Donald Greive (There are good tips in this secular 117-page booklet.)

Nurturing Reflective Christians to Teach: A Valiant Role for the Nation's Christian Colleges and Universities, edited by Daniel C. Elliott

"Renewing Integrity: A Christian Worldview and Educational Practice," David Naugle, National Faculty Leadership Conference

(www.dbu.edu/naugle.papers.htm)

Teaching That Works: Strategies From Scripture for Classrooms Today, Cliff Schimmels

Websites

www.internet4classrooms.com/brain_teasers.htm: great starter ideas

www.edu.uleth.ca/runte/tests: examples on how to design a test/ assessment tools

Learning to Write Objectives

edtech.Tennessee.edu/~bobannon/writing_objectives.html

www.personal.psu.edu/staff/b/x/bxbl1/Objectives/edweb.sdsu.edu/ Courses/EDTEC540/objectives/ObjectivesHome.html

meded.ucsd.edu/faculty/writing_instructional_objectives.pdf

Teaching Strategies

www.cmu.edu/teaching/trynew/index.html

www.ic.Arizona.edu/ic/edtech/strategy.html

teaching.Berkeley.edu/bgd/collaborative.html

www.videoprofessor.com/resourcelibrary/presentationskills/ improvepowerpointpresentationskills.html

www.thiagi.com/interactive-lectures.html

Questions and Critical Thinking

www.criticalthinking.org/

www.sfcp.org/uk/socratic_dialogue.htm

www.sfcp.org/uk/guidelines.htm

www.officeport.com/edu/blooms.htm

REFERENCE LIST

Cruickshank, D. R., Bainer, D. L., & Metcalf, K. K. (1999). *The act of teaching.* Boston: McGraw-Hill College.

Elmer, D. (2000). Trust: A good start on crosscultural effectiveness. *Trinity World Forum, 25*(2), 1-4.

Slavin, R. E. (1990). *Cooperative learning: Theory, research, and practice.* Englewood Cliffs, NJ: Prentice Hall.

7

Qualities of Excellent Teachers

Competencies for Effective Teaching

Good teaching goes beyond teaching methods. In this chapter are some important attributes of successful and effective teachers. Knowing these characteristics should provide practical insight as you begin your overseas teaching assignment.

GOOD TEACHERS KNOW WHAT THEY ARE TEACHING

Good teachers are masters of their subject area and are able to communicate this knowledge to students. In chapter five, we saw that Jesus knew what he taught and used that knowledge to challenge others to think in ways they never before considered.

Good teachers know their subject very well and are able to present the content in a way that is relevant to students' interests and needs. Good teachers teach courses in a manner that is valuable to students. Furthermore, when teachers possess comprehensive knowledge of the subject, they are more aware of misconceptions students are likely to have or develop about the subject (Cruickshank et al., 1999).

Things to Consider:

- What culturally relevant examples can be used in lectures that will better explain concepts in your subject matter to students?

- Think about ways you can model the thinking process in your field. Show students and then let them practice.

- Remember learning itself is humbling. Don't embarrass your students but develop trust so learning becomes more effective.

GOOD TEACHERS KNOW
HOW TO TEACH THEIR SUBJECT

Instructional strategies involve techniques, methods, materials and other means that are used to assist a student to achieve an educational goal. Examples of instructional strategies include activating prior knowledge, using appropriate reinforcement and practice, implementing cooperative learning, creating graphic organizers and applying efficient note-taking skills.

When teachers have a good understanding of teaching, they are better suited to select and implement instructional strategies that best meet students' learning needs (Cruickshank et al., 1999). Good teachers are concerned about the quality of their teaching. They understand that effective teaching does not just happen, but is a well-planned and thought-out endeavor. Good teachers communicate their subject in an organized, concise and clear manner. They organize their lessons well and explain concepts clearly, providing culturally relevant examples when possible (see appendix A for a lesson plan template). They state objectives, use a variety of instructional strategies, summarize major points, assess students to determine if they are learning and provide feedback to students so they can learn.

Things to Consider:

- Visuals and handouts can greatly support students' learning activities.

- Connect the academic content of the curriculum with the cultural context, especially for EFL learners. Example: *You are teaching business in Afghanistan and are explaining the principle of supply and demand. Kabul has a street that is just for selling tea. All the vendors selling tea line up right next to each other. Explain that a vendor might get a better price for his tea if he moves his booth to a part of town where there is no tea sold. Supply tea in a part of town where the demand is greatest and you will sell more tea and probably get a better price.* Consider how to make examples relevant to students' lives.

- In what areas do you need to improve the way you plan and organize lessons?

- Alternative teaching methods (projects, student presentations, films) that move beyond lectures facilitate active learning. What can I use? (See "Teaching Methods and Learning Styles" in appendix C.)

- What type of graphic organizers might fit my subject area and help students to learn?

GOOD TEACHERS ARE CREDIBLE AND TRUSTWORTHY

Knight (2006) points out that credible teachers have trustworthiness, having the best interests of the students at heart. Trustworthy teachers are sensitive to cultural issues, honest, friendly and kind. They strive to be fair and explain to students why certain decisions are made.

> Credibility and trust are the result of being open, honest, and equitable in your dealings with students, and of openly soliciting and accepting students' comments or criticisms, of defining

A *graphic organizer* is a visual and graphic display that depicts the relationships between facts, terms and/or ideas within a learning task such as knowledge maps, concept maps, story maps, cognitive organizers, advance organizers or concept diagrams.

your expectations and the relevance of the subject, of communicating clearly, and of demonstrating interest and concern for your students' success. As you can see, credibility and trust must be earned. (Cruickshank et al., 1999, p. 313)

Respect and trust must be earned. This may take longer in a distant classroom than in a North American or British classroom. Students might not trust foreign teachers, and you need to be aware that they will be watching you and your actions closely. Be patient and deliberate in developing credibility.

Problem and Solution Map

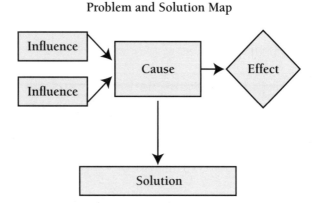

Figure 4. Problem and solution map. (Available, along with other graphic organizers, at http://www.cast.org/publications/ncac/ncac_go.html. Copyright, CAST. Used with permission.)

Sandy S., Ph.D., Music/Composition, Brazil

Adriane is a young woman who came to study violin with me here at the university. She already played quite well, but the school offers this course so cheaply that she decided to see if she could better her skills. After her second lesson, she began to open up and tell me about herself. She had lost her first husband the same day her first child was born; he was killed in a construction accident. She had become bitter and withdrawn from society until she met another young man. Not knowing much about him, but desperate for love and affection, she moved in with him and quickly discovered that he was an alcoholic. She was so angry with God she decided to get back at him by going to church and making fun of people. But the more she went to church, the more she felt a calming of her spirit. Her boyfriend decided to go with her to church, and he stopped drinking (it has been two years now since he's had alcohol). He asked her to marry him, but she said no. She is afraid.

When she came to me, she had decided to play her violin again after eight years of withdrawal from the instrument. When she discovered that I was a Christian, she was shocked. She said she knew then the Lord had brought her here, to me. After that we began to have serious discussions. She now plays in my orchestra and studies the violin with me, and she regularly comes for counseling. She finally reached the point where she asked me outright, "How can I be saved?" I carefully explained to her what it takes and gave her my own testimony. She is moving toward a commitment to Christ, and I believe that soon both she and the young man will become Christians and get married. I truly feel that God has a very special purpose for this young woman.

Things to Consider:

- Trust is vital in the teacher-student relationship. Don't ever lose sight of this.

- Again, don't talk about students with other students or with colleagues.

- Make sure to do what you say you will do. If you tell a student you will find some particular information for them, make sure you do it! Follow through on promises.

- Treat students equally. Avoid showing favoritism.

GOOD TEACHERS ARE FLEXIBLE

The most effective teachers are prepared for and able to adapt to a variety of circumstances (Walberg, 1990). Good teachers are aware of the need for change, understand what change is required and are willing to change. This includes adapting instruction and classroom routines. Good teaching is not always about your planned agenda. It is about deviating from the course syllabus or lecture when teachable moments arise. You must take advantage of teachable moments because they can lead to in-depth life lessons.

For example, you may be teaching a class on how to do graduate-level research for Western universities. You've planned three hours on the topic of plagiarism and citing sources. A student asks why this is so important in the West. You explain that it is wrong to steal intellectual property. Plagiarism is stealing. Then a student says, "Well, stealing isn't always wrong." And there you have a teachable moment. This is a time to lay aside your first agenda and teach to the moment. A flexible attitude is important not only for your mindset but also for students who expect you to be in charge of any situation. Good teaching is flexible in order to meet students' needs.

Things to Consider:

- When your instruction plan doesn't seem to be working, determine why and implement an alternative strategy. Plan B can be your best friend in a tough situation.

- Read your audience: Are they bored, lost, anxious? How are they adjusting in the middle of the lesson? The inability to answer questions well, failure to complete a task, or puzzled or frustrated faces may indicate that there is a lack of understanding and therefore a lack of learning.

- When planning lessons, keep in mind individual learning differences and cultural factors and consider alternative methods.

GOOD TEACHERS PROMOTE
ACTIVE LEARNING IN STUDENTS

Education is an active process, and good teachers provide opportunities for students to share their knowledge and experiences. Chickering and Gamson (1987) suggest that students must do more than just listen: they must read, write, discuss or be engaged in solving problems of some sort. The key to good teaching and learning is active participation by the learner in the process. Good teachers use teaching methods that engage students and promote active learning. They encourage students to participate and provide them with opportunities to talk about a whole host of concepts, issues and struggles. They motivate students by sparking interest and revealing relevance. They encourage student questions, opinions and discussion. Instead of just giving students information, they seek to have students discover some of the knowledge. Make sure students are challenged and encouraged rather than bored and uninterested.

Things to Consider:

- Active learning involves observing, doing and dialoging. What assignments and activities can be used to get students involved in learning by engaging these three areas?

- Brief activities introduced into the lecture will help students remember more content. How can you introduce student activity into your lectures? You may insert brief demonstrations or short writing exercises followed by class discussion. This goes back to the principle of teaching in intervals.

- Journaling, group work, questions and discussion can be used to actively engage students in your subject area. How can you integrate these into your plans?

- Resistance may come from students who are not familiar or comfortable with active learning. What will you do to reduce this resistance?

- Practical, relevant applications for new knowledge are vital. Lack of this application leads to lower student motivation. What can you do to help students use newly acquired knowledge in their everyday lives?

- Consider how to interact more, lecture less and emphasize active learning.

GOOD TEACHERS HAVE HIGH EXPECTATIONS

Good teachers hold high expectations for themselves and their students. They believe all students can learn, and they have the ability to help all students learn. Research informs us that when teachers' expectations of students rise, students learn more. Teacher expectations affect student outcomes because the actions teachers take are in response to their expectations (Good & Brophy, 2000). Good teachers communicate high expectations to students and help each student to attain success. Teachers' expectations of students must be reasonable and modified frequently.

Keep in mind that teachers communicate expectations in many subtle ways. For example, a teacher might be willing to wait on a student who he thinks will respond with a correct answer while skipping over a student he believes will not succeed. Students pick up on these subtleties and may categorize classmates as smart and not-so-smart. Worse, the student that is quickly skipped over may begin to view himself this way as well.

Things to Consider:

- How am I communicating my expectations to students?

- Do my students' cultural differences affect my expectations for them?

- Do I lower my expectations to an appropriate level for students for whom English is a foreign language?

- How can I gain student input about reasonable expectations and goals?

- Remediation is sometimes needed. What are some possible ways I can plan for this?

- Students improve. Do not always center on perfection, but rather growth and progress.

- Am I getting to know my students well enough to set more realistic expectations?

GOOD TEACHERS CREATE A POSITIVE LEARNING ENVIRONMENT

Good teachers are aware of the physical and psychological environment of the classroom and can manipulate these two elements to increase learning (Anderson, 1991). Teachers can use seating arrangements, bulletin boards and other physical aspects of the room to promote a more positive learning environment. Good teachers also recognize the need to make the classroom comfortable and nonthreatening so students are willing to contribute to class discussion, including asking questions and sharing ideas and experiences from their own lives. Students need to know that they are important and invited to participate.

Positive classroom climate requires good teachers to have a genuine interest in students and to respect and relate to students as individuals. They care that students are learning and are concerned about the welfare of students. They use positive language rather than focusing on the negative. Find genuine ways to affirm your students.

Good teachers build learning communities. When teachers build a community in their classrooms, students respond positively. When teachers are approachable, friendly, available and willing to help students both in and out of the classroom, this also contributes to a positive classroom climate.

Linette C., M.A., TEFL, Asia

One of my favorite parts of teaching here is holding office hours. My students love to come practice their English, learn about American culture and find out how I feel about their culture. Our free-flowing talks range over many topics, and they regularly touch on spiritual matters. I think my record attendance at an office hour was twenty-five students (we had to meet outside!). On an average week I might have forty to fifty students spread out over six office hours. Some come only sporadically, but many come every week. These times are not only an invaluable language- and culture-learning opportunity for my students, but they give me a chance to share a little bit of my life with them.

Things to Consider:

- Deliberate, thoughtful planning can create a positive learning environment.

- Arrive at class early and stay late. Talk with your students.

- Post and keep office hours. This might be strange to students and may take some time for them to get accustomed to.

- Pay attention to the physical setting.

- Use positive reinforcement with students.

- In order to create a positive learning environment, you should communicate your expectations to your students each day.

GOOD TEACHERS ENJOY TEACHING

Good teachers have what Knight (2006) terms "dynamism." An excellent teacher has a passion for teaching. These teachers are energetic and enthusiastic about their subject and love to teach. Not only does enthusiasm make a course more enjoyable, but students retain

---

Bill W., J.D., Law, Asia

We hold regular "office hours" in our apartment for each of my classes. During the vast majority of these times, nothing of great significance happens. One week, though, something different happened. We had our regular Tuesday night visit with a group of graduate students to whom I taught constitutional law last semester. Most have been here twenty-five times this year, never showing much interest in spiritual things. They asked me to answer this question: "Why are you a Christian?" We had a great discussion and one promised to read the book of John, then discuss it with me in September. He is one of the most enthusiastic Communist Party members we know. We look forward to seeing how God will be at work in his life.

---

more information when the teacher is excited about the subject matter. Students are more likely to develop enthusiasm of their own and to achieve higher levels of learning (Good & Brophy, 2000).

Things to Consider:

- Be enthusiastic about teaching. If you are not excited about teaching, then why should students be excited about learning?

- Be passionate about your subject and excited to teach others about it.

- Be flexible and willing to change to increase students' interest.

- Think about how you can change the pace of the class by using a variety of teaching strategies.

- Evaluate your nonverbal communication. Provide nonverbal encouragement and maintain eye contact when it is culturally appropriate.

GOOD TEACHERS KNOW THEIR STUDENTS AND DEVELOP POSITIVE RELATIONSHIPS WITH THEM

What separates novices from experienced teachers is that new teachers lack in-depth knowledge of their students. In order to choose ef-

Olga A., Ph.D., Russian Language and Culture, Asia

I have one student who is really close to my heart now. Her name is LX. Last year in her composition she wrote that she had no interest in studying and even thought that if she would take her life, nobody would be upset. The number of suicides in universities here is high. I invited her to my home to talk. She told me that her mom died one year ago after being sick for a long time. After a few months her father remarried, and her stepmother hates her and constantly reproaches her because the family has to spend too much money on her education. LX stopped communicating with her father and didn't want to go home even for holidays. She attended the university without any drive or ambition.

She asked me why I have an optimistic view of life, and I told her about my personal relationship with God. She started to come to my home more often and told me about her thoughts, feelings and concerns. Sometimes she came to me for advice and support. I realized she lacked love and care from people. She started to read the Bible and she had a lot of questions. She started to go to church with me. One day she said she wanted to become a Christian and she believes in the Bible. She accepted the Lord.

Many people can tell that LX became a new person in these past two years since we met! Now she is joyful and usually has a cheerful mood. Being her teacher, I can witness that even her attitude toward studying changed completely. I was touched very much by her words to me one day: "When I will be in heaven with my Father, I will look for you there to say 'Thank you!'" And this is the same person who was thinking about taking her life two years ago!

fective teaching methods and help students learn, you must first know something about the students you are teaching.

Good teachers establish a rapport with students. Building relationships with students based on trust, respect and authentic caring will give you the rapport that good teachers seek. Crosscultural teaching requires that teachers relate to and understand people of different races, cultures and social class backgrounds. Garcia (1991) points out that contact in interpersonal relationships must be meaningful and should foster better understanding of and empathy for students' feelings, beliefs and cultural differences.

Things to Consider:

- How will you learn and understand your students' cultural backgrounds and experiences so you can use that knowledge productively in the teaching-learning process?

- The invisible diversity is an underlying factor and a constant in the crosscultural classroom. Be aware that many issues not immediately apparent influence how students respond to you as an instructor, especially in crosscultural situations, such as female instructors in a Middle Eastern context.

- Questionnaires, casual visits, listening, observation or asking for their autobiographies will help you learn about your students.

- Use e-mail to increase accessibility to your students.

- Spend time with students outside of class. Take students to lunch.

- While in China, Mike played Ping-Pong every day after class with students and followed up with taking some of them to lunch. Several students and colleagues would show up for these afternoons together. There were numerous opportunities to discuss a variety of issues related to the class as well as their personal or spiritual concerns. Be accessible.

GOOD TEACHERS ARE SERVANTS
TO STUDENTS AND COLLEAGUES

As Christian educators, we must be ambassadors for Christ. That means serving others. Serving starts with an attitude of giving. Pat Gustin (Baumgartner et al., 2002) lists several aspects of an attitude of service:

- We consider others as our equals, accepting the role of a learner.

- We become servants, giving up our rights to be "in charge."

- We cast our lot with those around us, experiencing life as they do as much as possible.

- We try to see the world through their eyes, rather than asking them to look through ours.

- We choose to see the good around us, cultivating a sense of tolerance and ultimate acceptance.

- We admit that our own culture is less than perfect.

Things to Consider:

- Be available and offer your help. People often need help with a variety of tasks. When you can, offer your assistance. That can mean ordering a book for a student who has no access to outside resources, editing a paper for a faculty colleague, helping someone move or helping a colleague solve a computer problem.

- Answer students' questions and help with their research or English language development. Students have many questions that need to be addressed.

- Be humble.

- Build a library. Bring as many books as you can and leave as many as you can. Think about the perspectives presented in the books you choose. Donate your books to the school's library. Students will quickly start using the books and ask many questions.

- Conduct English Corners. In some countries students have a sincere desire to develop their English-speaking abilities. In such cases students are willing to talk about anything just as long as they hear and speak English. Give them a place to do that.

- Look for your students' and colleagues' needs and serve them in a Christlike manner.

William W., Ph.D., Christianity and Comparative Religions, Asia

As I was celebrating Mid-Autumn Festival with my students on the campus lawn, another group of students decided to join us. I invited them to my English Club. Jamie came with questions, and one night I spent two hours reasoning with her about God's existence and the beauty of Jesus. "Ask God to show himself to you," I said. She walked away unconvinced but desperately searching. The semester ended. Jamie disappeared into the city's vast millions, and I didn't hear from her again until I received this e-mail in December:

Dear William: About one year ago, we discussed about the God and you told me to ask HIM. Recently, God finally find me! How happy and thankful I am! So I want to share this good news with you! You are one of those lovely people who led me to God. Thank you! Wish you peace and Happy Christmas! Yours, J.

GOOD TEACHERS HAVE A SENSE OF HUMOR

An "appropriate" sense of humor is a characteristic students enjoy in teachers (Csikszentmihalyi & McCormack, 1986). Humor can reduce tension, communicate the teacher's confidence and promote trust (Cruickshank et al., 1999). Used appropriately, humor can motivate students and develop group cohesion. It can make you appear more human to your students. Laughing with your class is important in creating a pleasant and productive environment.

Things to Consider:

- The safest target for humor is yourself, not your students. This prevents them from feeling threatened.

- Fit your humor into your style and subject. Share funny stories from your life that demonstrate important concepts.

- Different cultures respond to humor in different ways. Humor must be appropriate. If you are not sure, clear it with a national you trust before you use it.

- Sarcasm is an area of humor that will create problems. Many students will not understand that your sarcastic remarks are only meant in jest, and these can hurt them. It is probably best to stay away from sarcasm.

- Use humor in a natural way that fits your personality and your comfort level.

GOOD TEACHERS PRAY FOR THEIR STUDENTS

Earlier we discussed how Jesus prayed for his students. It is important in a crosscultural setting to pray for your students. You might be the only person praying for that student by name. Prayer is an essential part of your walk with Christ. Without a regular prayer life, your teaching and witness will be less effective and you will be more vulnerable to the enemy. Prayer is vital in discerning and doing God's will. You and your students need prayer.

Things to Consider:

Here are a few things teachers can pray about:

- Pray for wisdom (Jas 1:5) to discern what doors to walk through and what opportunities to grasp.

- Pray to be given insight about the seeking hearts of your students and fellow teachers.

- Pray that their eyes, ears and hearts are open.

- Pray for the conversion of your students and colleagues. Pray for their salvation.

- Pray for wisdom in your teaching in order to meet students' needs.

In some countries these teacher attributes may seem unusual or strange. That is good because it will cause students to seek answers and will provide opportunities for you to talk with them about Christ, who has made the difference in your life.

GOING DEEPER, GOING FURTHER

Suggested Readings

College Teaching Abroad: A Handbook of Strategies for Successful Cross-cultural Exchanges, Pamela Gale George (secular)

Educating for Shalom: Essays on Christian Higher Education, Nicholas Wolterstorff, edited by Clarence W. Joldersma and Gloria Goris Stronks

The 4-MAT System: Teaching to Learning Styles with Right/Left Mode Techniques, Bernice McCarthy

Frames of Mind: The Theory of Multiple Intelligences, Howard Gardner

Gladly Learn, Gladly Teach: Living Out One's Calling in the Twenty-First Century Academy, John Marson Dunaway, editor

How People Learn Brain, Mind, Experience and School: Expanded Edition, published through the NRCC on Learning Research and Educational Practice

To Know as We Are Known: Education as a Spiritual Journey, Parker J. Palmer

Ministering in the Secular University: A Guide for Christian Professors and Staff, Joseph M. Mellichamp

Multiple Intelligences: Theory in Practice–A Reader, Howard Gardner

Pedagogy of the Heart, Paulo Freire

Films on Good Teaching

Stand and Deliver (1988) PG *Hispanic/African American*

Freedom Writers (2007) PG-13 *African American/Hispanic*

Websites

www.unesco.org: information on education worldwide

www.learning-styles-online.com/inventory: inventories for students' learning styles

REFERENCE LIST

Anderson, L. W. (1991). Classroom environment and climate. *Increasing teacher effectiveness.* Paris: UNESCO. www.unesco.org

Baumgartner, E. W., Dybdahl, J. L., Gustin, P., & Moyer, B. C. (2002). *Passport to mission* (2nd ed.). Andrews University, Berrien Springs, MI: Institute of World Mission.

Chickering, A. W., & Gamson, Z. F. (1987). Seven principles for good practice. *AAHE Bulletin 39:* 3-7.

Cruickshank, D. R., Bainer, D. L., & Metcalf, K. K. (1999). *The Act of Teaching.* Boston: McGraw-Hill College.

Csikszentmihalyi, M., & McCormack, J. (1986). The influence of teachers. *Phi Delta Kappan, 67*(6), 415-19.

Garcia, R. L. (1991). *Teaching in a pluralistic society: Concepts, model, strategies* (2nd ed.). New York: HarperCollins.

Good, T. L., & Brophy, J. E. (2000). *Looking in classrooms* (8th ed.).New York: Longman.

Knight, A. B. (2006). Teacher credibility: A tool for diagnosing problems in teacher/student relationships. From http://www.ou.edu/pii/tips/ideas/credibility.html.

Walberg, H. J. (1990). Productive teaching and instruction: Assessing the knowledge base. *Phi Delta Kappan Journal, 7*(6), 470-78.

8

Hey, I Didn't Sign Up for This!

Expectations and Accommodations

Ni hao, Mr. Xu! It's Mike Romanowski." Mike speaks into the phone very slowly and carefully. "Well, there's a lot of *shui* [Mike fervently hopes this is Chinese for "water"] standing in our bathroom. Yes. Water is standing in our bathroom." He pauses. "A lot. No, it is very difficult to use the bathroom because there is so much water in there. Can you please send someone to take a look at it? Xìe xìe." Mike's sure that means "thank you."

Mr. Xu is the International Affairs Officer assigned to help with university housing for all foreign professors. As Mike hangs up, uncertain if Mr. Xu *really* understood his request, he tells his wife, Janet, "They are either sending a plumber, bringing more drinking water, or I have a package at the post office." Communicating cross-culturally can have its challenges.

Mike and his family moved to China from Ohio to work and live among university students because they had a sense of calling to that place. They wanted to share God's love with Chinese students. Now this family of six was trying to figure out what to do with all the water standing on their bathroom floor. Two inches of water is more than just an inconvenience. In an apartment that has no heat and winter temperatures hovering around 35 degrees F, it's a health hazard.

Within a few hours, Mr. Xu sends a plumber. The plumber looks at the situation, pulls out a wrench, makes some noise and declares that there is absolutely nothing wrong. He explains that he has no idea where the water is coming from. Nothing is broken; nothing needs fixing. After some discussion (some in Chinese, some in English), Mike is told that the problem is *condensation*. The plumber packs up his toolbox and heads back to the office. The two inches of water is still there and remains there for the next six months.

Mike and his family expected difficulties in communicating. They expected adjustments when it came to food, cultural norms and even in their living conditions. But nothing had prepared them for a bathroom turned into an ice rink and a plumber who declared nothing was broken while standing in water. When it came time for payment, the plumber would not take any money but simply asked if his payment might be allowing his children to play with the four American children for one hour each day. A relationship was formed.

Song of Solomon says that the little foxes ruin the vineyards (Song 2:15). It's true—the unexpected, inconvenient little things can destroy a person's motivation and drive while living and serving overseas.

Little foxes are things like not receiving the class roster until the end of the semester, only to realize that out of the sixty students whose papers you've painstakingly graded, only twenty-five were actually signed up for the class. Or going to class to give your students their final exam and finding that another teacher has taken your classroom because he thought it was better for test taking—squatter's rights. It is the unpredictable like showing up for class prepared with a carefully honed lesson, only to learn that your students are gone for four weeks picking potatoes somewhere in Ukraine.

When a person teaches in a distant classroom, she needs to be prepared that all hell *will* break loose. Trouble comes from the most unexpected places. We can guarantee that what you expected when you signed up for your crosscultural teaching assignment and what you will actually face will be completely and totally different. Every teacher moving overseas arrives with preconceived ideas about what it will be like, and these expectations color each person's experiences. Whether it is the condition of the classroom, how students learn or water standing in your bathroom, teachers' predetermined notions clash with the realities they face once there—both *inside* and *outside* of the classroom.

False expectations cause more anxiety and stress in crosscultural settings than anything else. Expectations provide us with a form of false assurance that sets us up for an abrupt fall into reality and disappointment. Some never recover and head back home—emotionally shipwrecked. But two important questions can help you in preparing:

1. Are you aware of the expectations you hold?

2. How will you cope when expectations collide with reality?

Let's examine some of the common expectations teachers take with them as they cross borders, and explore some suggestions on how to cope when reality moves in.

EXPECTATIONS ABOUT STUDENTS

Teachers moving into crosscultural classrooms often embrace several of the following student expectations.

Knowledge. "My students will be advanced in their knowledge and understanding." Teachers naturally begin their overseas teaching with assumptions about their students' prior knowledge and academic background. Teachers expect students will be very informed about the subject matter, generally at the level they were during their educational endeavors. They assume the content should be taught at an advanced level.

Reality check: In many crosscultural classrooms, it is common for new teachers to discover that students lack the prior knowledge needed to understand the subject matter. Often upper-level courses become introductory courses out of sheer necessity. In some cases, especially in emerging or developing nations, graduate courses are frequently taught the way North American universities teach under-graduate courses. This is not a reflection on students' intelligence or on their eagerness to learn, but rather a commentary on the scarcity of good educational resources. In nations with Internet restrictions and few library books, the majority of graduate students have never written a research paper in their entire academic careers. It is nearly

---

Robert L., Ph.D., Christian Studies, Gindiri, Plateau State, Nigeria

I believe that our faithful God brought me here to this college to teach his Word and represent both a biblically relevant and passionate pastoral view of Christianity, especially in terms of a biblical worldview. I am so pleased that four of my third-year students have sought me out to have regular discipleship times of Bible study and prayer. They ask to borrow good books to read and drop by our apartment to visit. Another student, Israel, after taking my class on the biblical world of the Old Testament, expressed a desire to go to seminary after graduating from college. Others have come for help on biblical questions. Some say that if they go to their own pastors for questions, the pastor will think they are trying to espouse heresy. I think my neutrality as a university professor makes it easier for them to approach me with real theological questions.

My view of our mission here has changed since arriving in Nigeria. I thought I was coming to teach hundreds of eager students that were part of the exciting African revival, but that is not the case in Gindiri. The majority of students in our religion department think that religion is an easy way to graduate and get a teaching job—a wonderful goal in a poverty-stricken country like Nigeria, but a poor reason to study or teach the Bible. I cannot change the tide of nominal Christianity that is now present here, but by God's grace I hope to influence a few students significantly in terms of their walks with Christ and their attitudes about serving him.

---

impossible to determine the prior knowledge and background of students before entering their classroom. No matter what country, teachers should spend time early in the semester getting students ready for advanced work (Thurston et al., 1994).

Student motivation. "All my students will be eager to learn." It is true that many students outside of North America are motivated to learn, often more so than North American students. But teachers often cling to stereotypes of what overseas students will be like and how they will learn and how these students will positively respond to their teaching.

Reality check: Not all students *are* eager to learn. Some are at the university by default because of high unemployment rates in their country or because they were not certain what they wanted to do after secondary school. Also, not all students are enamored of foreign teachers. Be prepared that some students might resent you in their classroom.

English skills. "Since they want me to teach in English, I am certain all students in my classes will have good English listening, reading, writing and speaking skills."

Reality check: Most North Americans will be teaching in English regardless of the subject matter or academic discipline. Most teachers find the students' actual range of English skills varies greatly. Some students will grasp 90 percent of the lecture, while others will understand as little as 50 percent (Thurston et al., 1994), and still others, even less. Knowing the language and reading abilities of EFL students is important as you supplement your lectures to increase learning. Repeating major concepts, writing new vocabulary on the board and restating basic principles are necessary in a class where English is not your students' first language. This takes time and energy and restricts the amount of content that can be covered. The material you might be able to manage in an overseas context will often be about half what you could cover in a semester in a North American classroom.

Similarities. "Students around the world are pretty much alike and are aware of academic protocol and ethics." Teachers believe that students are committed to the same ethical ideals regarding plagiarism and cheating.

Reality check: It is important to understand that other cultures view the world much differently than you do, and this affects the classroom dramatically. For example, the Western teacher who believes that punctuality is an unquestioned virtue has developed certain expectations for student behavior concerning time and might erroneously stereotype students who fail to exhibit that behavior as lazy and unmotivated, assuming they do not take their studies seriously. This teacher will have difficulty working with non-Western students who are much more relaxed about time and time constraints. These students may not regard punctuality as important and may believe deadlines are flexible and adaptable. Differences like this can hinder and frustrate the foreign instructor, especially if he lacks the ability to adapt.

Keep in mind that issues that you might consider standard are not at all that clear-cut in a distant land. For example, Mike spent hours reflecting on, teaching about and addressing the issue of plagiarism in both his Asian and Middle Eastern classrooms. Although in the U.S. there are consequences when a student breaks rules about plagiarism or not citing sources, these are viewed from a completely different perspective in other lands and cannot, at least at first, be handled from a Western point of view. In nations that allow and protect the piracy of intellectual property, plagiarism is an accepted form of work.

Then there is cheating. Socialism and communism have formed the worldviews of students in many nations, leaving them with no word for "cheating." In these cultures, all knowledge belongs to the people and at test time, all knowledge is to be shared. If I have the right answer to a hard test question and my classmate doesn't, it is my duty to provide my comrade with the right information. It's helping; it's life in community.

Brian B. taught business in Russia. He was frustrated by his students not getting his message about honesty and fulfilling obligations. Not only was cheating a problem, but students didn't fulfill assignments. Students were told they had a three-page paper due discussing a problem they might deal with regarding ethics in business. They wouldn't be allowed to take the final exam unless they turned in this paper. Each week leading up to the due date Brian reminded the class of the assignment. Then the due date came, two weeks before the final exam. Not one student turned in the assignment. Brian got very agitated and told the class again this was a requirement in order to take the final exam and pass the class. He gave them one more week to complete the paper.

The new due date came. Again, no one turned in the paper. Brian was ready to cancel the class and fail every student. Then a student came in late. Amazingly, he had completed the assignment. Brian was stunned. He pointed out to the class that this one student, the only one to turn in his paper, now had the opportunity to pass the class. Then an idea came to him. This was an opportunity to share the gospel. He said, "Here we have one person who did something that may save all of you from failing. As many of you know, I am a Christian. I believe the story of Jesus: one man, dying on the cross, to save many. Now we have an example of one person who has done something to help all of you. I am giving you one more week to complete the assignment because of what this one student has done. If you turn in the paper the day before the final, I'll allow you to take the exam. Just as Jesus saved many, you also have been saved by one."

The next week, all the students turned in the paper. They actually did a good job on them. When Brian asked the students why they finally did the assignment, one student stood up. "Mr. B., you were strict saying we had to complete the assignment. But you were such a nice professor we didn't believe you would actually make consequences for us. But when we saw last week that you were serious and that we would not pass the class, we were glad you gave us another chance. We took the time to complete the assignment. Thank you for your forgiveness."

The next day he gave the final exam. Finally, he did not have any students cheating. Afterward, he asked one of the students privately what had happened. He said, "Well, I think we are starting to get the idea of what you were teaching about ethics and honesty. We decided to give it a try, at least for your class."

Suggestions:
This is not a comprehensive list, but here are some additional ideas for getting through the rough spots and avoiding cultural collisions.

- Develop a short assignment at the start of each semester designed to assess the prior knowledge of students. For example, use a writing assignment in which students are asked several questions about education and their perceptions of education. Reading what your students write about these questions will provide valuable insight into their knowledge and perspectives. It also helps you assess their English-writing abilities, which will be useful in preparing future lessons and assignments.

- Before your arrival, plan a two-week introduction or preview section to provide students with the knowledge and the skills they will need to be successful in your class. Train, teach and prepare them for the expectations, goals and objectives you will have in class. And bring some materials with you. Don't assume anything is available in the host nation. In much of the world, students do not have access to textbooks, and university libraries have few resources.

- If possible, find resources to help you understand your future students: what they think about the world, how they learn, what goals they have, who their heroes are. Try to talk with others who have taught in the country in which you will be serving.

- Be prepared for the worst when it comes to the students' language abilities. There are several ways to improve the comprehension level of students in your classes (see chapters six, seven and ten).

- Realize your own cultural fingerprints (Baumgartner et al., 2002). North Americans are time-oriented and some cultures are not. Americans are task-oriented while other cultures may focus more on social interaction. (Mike's plumber was more interested in a relationship than fixing the leak.) American culture is individualistic while other cultures admire and promote community. Different cultures learn in different ways. Thinking processes vary between cultures, so use relevant pedagogies that connect the culture of the students to the culture of the classroom and the knowledge being presented. For example, discussion and questions are cherished in Western classrooms while Eastern students are taught to simply listen to lectures. Westerners value linear thinking while Easterners are more cyclical in their approaches to ideas. This does not mean you cannot use discussion, but you need to be aware of differences and help your students learn new ways of learning. Above all else, adapt.

- Most importantly, relax. Pray and trust that God has called you to this place and will help you adjust. Ask him to open your eyes and ears to learn so that you might be a good teacher in a distant classroom.

EXPECTATIONS ABOUT
CLASSROOMS AND FACILITIES

Western teachers' preconceived ideas about what their classrooms will be like are understandably based on their experience teaching in Western classrooms. These usually center on the following assumptions:

- Since teaching and schools are not effective unless equipped with adequate technology and supplies (by North American standards), my overseas classroom will probably have basic technology and adequate materials.

- The classroom, copy machine, support staff, my office and the computer equipment will all be adequate for my teaching.

- I'll be assigned a classroom and it will be unlocked during regular school hours.

- Electricity will be on during the day.

- Students will have desks and textbooks.

- I will have a class roster.
- Classrooms will be clean and well stocked.

Reality:

Teaching conditions and resources will most likely vary from nation to nation, university to university, department to department and even classroom to classroom.

- Some classrooms may have a computer and video projector to show your PowerPoint slides. In others chalk may be your only technology. Don't panic. Remember that Jesus was an excellent teacher and had neither technology nor chalk.

- You might get a private office or share with others.

- Class rosters and academic calendars, common at colleges and universities in North America, are frequently missing in universities overseas.

- Resources and materials might be difficult to find, and duplication of your class notes might even be impossible. Much depends on the particular country and university.

- Some instructors find there aren't enough desks in the classroom for all of their students. This means spending a good portion of class time hunting and gathering enough seats for everyone, just to find that next class period you're back in the same predicament.

- In some cultures, keys are a sign of power and may be the only control the key holder has over anything in his life. This means that classrooms can be locked, and finding the one who holds the keys isn't easy. And once he's found, he may not be willing to trek across campus to unlock a room.

An American law professor e-mailed friends: "It's time for the spring semester to begin. The students performed well on the winter exams and we were happy to see them display a strong grasp of the material. Academic logistics are a problem here in Romania. **Please pray** that we can work out good class schedules (with classrooms!)

for the new semester. Since the three Common Law courses are optional, we have to work them in between the mandatory classes and it can be extremely challenging to get a decent arrangement. The first week is consumed with meeting with the students to work this all out. We know this seems mundane, but it makes a big difference as to how well the semester goes."

Things at the host university may seem chaotic, and you might find yourself wondering, *How does learning ever take place here?* But it does. Things do have a way of working themselves out.

Suggestions:

Teachers in distant classrooms must adapt their teaching style and make accommodations—sometimes spontaneously. You may not be able to rely on technology, and your home computer may not be compatible with your classroom. Be prepared for power outages and have a low-tech lesson available as a backup. You may need to bring adapters and cables from home for your computer, and make sure everything you buy is dual voltage. You can usually purchase electrical strips overseas and probably will find some of your computer supplies available, but we suggest bringing all essential items because it takes time to find particulars in the new culture. Also be aware of the compatibility of your DVDs or VCRs. Check to see what system the country uses. Many DVDs from North America won't play on overseas systems.

If at all possible, visit your classroom prior to your first day of class to check out the computer system, lighting, desks and anything else needed for the lesson. Find the building maintenance person, sometimes known as the "Key Holder," and make sure you have a nice gift for him to show your appreciation (such as a ball cap of a famous sports team, a nice T-shirt with a U.S. university logo or a box of candy). University machinery outside of North America often runs on this type of lubrication. It never hurts to say "thank you" in advance.

It is vitally important to get to know your new city and look for alternative sources for things like copies and office supplies. The bottom line is this: assess what you *must* have for your teaching, at least for those first few weeks. Bring as many resources as you need, but bring them on CDs or thumb drives and just a few hard copies. Don't take up a lot of space in your suitcase, but you need to be prepared for your first few classes. All of this allows you to be as self-sufficient as possible until you learn the lay of the land and what is available in your host culture. Find substitutes when items are impossible to find. Life can go on without Post-it notes.

EXPECTATIONS ABOUT LIVING CONDITIONS

Often teachers accept an overseas position with a somewhat distorted sense of what their living conditions might be like. It is doubtful that any expect luxury accommodations, but most do expect at least the same efficient access to public utilities that they are accustomed to in their home country. In many countries these assumptions are mistaken:

- I will have sufficient living conditions.
- I will have hot water for bathing and for washing clothes.
- Everyone has easily obtained high-speed Internet access.
- I can get a cell phone without any difficulty.
- Can't wait to get cable or satellite TV! I should be able to watch the Super Bowl, right?
- I have the right to privacy of my e-mail, phone conversations and regular mail.

Reality:
Public services differ greatly throughout the world. Moving from a place where water, electricity and sanitation are easily accessible to a place where services are not reliable requires a vast adjustment. In addition, simply trying to get services in your apartment can be very time consuming. You may be exposed to corrupt officials who administer services with an unspoken request for a gift to move things along.

Lack of privacy is one of the most difficult adjustments for teachers coming from North America. It is not uncommon for communist nations, countries in the Middle East and even some European nations to look at your e-mails, check which websites you're visiting and even read your regular post mail. In some countries teachers regularly have others listening in on their telephone conversations. Teri once had an overseas school administrator congratulate her on her sister's pregnancy as he handed her an opened letter from home announcing the good news! Teachers crossing borders must be prepared to give up some of their civil rights that are taken for granted in the West. Be prepared. Brace yourself. Remember that Jesus gave up all of his rights to come and live among the human race. It's tough, but not impossible.

EXPECTATIONS ABOUT FACULTY

Teachers entering distant classrooms often arrive with several wrong expectations about workloads and courses:

- I will teach courses that are directly in my field of study.

- My colleagues will appreciate my contribution to the department and be glad I am here.

- A syllabus is a standard for all universities.

- The academic calendar will be readily available upon my request and it will tell me the holiday schedule, days off and examination dates.

- I will be handed a contract and class schedule the day I arrive on campus.

Reality:

Teaching workloads in distant classrooms vary substantially from one institution to another and even from one program to another.

- Be prepared to teach outside your discipline or a course that you have never taught before. Scripture tells us to be prepared in season and out of season (2 Tim 4:2).

- Stay ready—you might not know what you're teaching, when you're teaching or even who you are teaching.

- Most crosscultural teachers report that they do far more than simply teach assigned classes. Additional work can include editing English professional papers for a colleague, correcting department documents translated into English, providing workshops, giving weekly all-campus lectures, engaging in research collaboration, assisting students with research papers or a whole host of other possibilities.

- Be open to good opportunities and wise to those that are not fruitful.

- Class sizes also vary greatly but tend to be much larger than the norm in North America.

- Try to protect yourself from being naive. Not everyone on your university campus is thrilled to see you there. Occasionally colleagues and even students might see you as a threat. Did you take a job from a national? Are there anti-U.S. sentiments hovering around? Is your native-English tongue making others uncomfortable and fearful their English skills will be discovered to be less than adequate? Don't be surprised by rejection within your department. It happens.

- Contracts, class schedules and academic calendars are often neglected in other cultures. Don't freak out. The lack of these items has nothing to do with you. It's just a part of the way the system functions.

Suggestions:

- Approach your teaching assignment assuming that your workload will be very heavy. If it is heavy, then you are ready. If it is a lighter load then you will be surprised and can pursue other activities.

- Make your own class roster. It's a great way to get to know students' names.

- Befriend a colleague within the university system who will let you know of important dates, holidays off and any meetings you might need to attend. Things have a way of working out.

- Guard your time and do not become overcommitted. Choose wisely the work you want to accept beyond the classroom and learn how to say no in a culturally appropriate manner. Saying no (in a caring manner) is not being a poor Christian witness. Doing poor quality work because of being overcommitted *is* a poor witness, so learn to make good decisions about how you spend your time.

- Talk with colleagues about which tasks you should accept. Some requests are not as important as others. For example, if your department head asks you to help write a proposal that will get grant money for the entire department, that has the potential of being a benefit to the whole department and the university. Contrast that task to a neighbor who wants you to help him write to a U.S. newspaper complaining about U.S. policy in the Middle East. Prioritizing is tough and it needs to be done prayerfully and very intentionally. Each person matters, but some tasks are too time consuming and zap you of much-needed energy for other more strategic tasks.

- Be willing to do the dirty stuff that no one else wants, but try to be wise. Heed Jesus' words in Matthew 10:16 about being as wise as serpents but as gentle as doves. Be discerning and learn the expectations that your school, your colleagues and your students have of you.

- Understand that your teaching is the number-one priority. Time for class preparation and meeting with students must be guarded. No matter what the workload is, make sure the preparation time needed to develop solid lessons is not pushed aside in order to perform other duties.

EXPECTATIONS ABOUT DAILY LIFE

The West likes to plan ahead. Most of us from North America believe there are certain rules about living that should be followed. Everyone in the world has similar rules and plans ahead, don't they? Here are a few assumptions that Westerners cling to.

- I will be informed in advance when people want to visit my home.

- Most countries adhere to the 9 and 9 rule: never call anyone before 9 a.m. or after 9 p.m. unless it's an emergency.

- I will be notified in advance when I am invited to formal or informal events.

- Working from a list is the most efficient way to get things accomplished. Everyone knows the more I accomplish, the better I am.

Reality:
Western cultural rules about planning ahead are hardly even noted in other cultures. North Americans give ample notice for dinner engagements. However, many countries are not as concerned about planning (or not as *obsessed* with planning) as North Americans. For example, Mike once was called at 2:00 p.m. to give a lecture at 6:00 p.m., and had visitors phone at 7:00 a.m. for their 8:00 a.m. visit. Many cultures are more concerned with the human aspects of social interaction and place little or no emphasis on efficiency. As a result systems run on a different timetable. Tasks or activities that in your home culture might have taken you an hour to accomplish may take all day in your new host culture. In many countries, especially in the developing world, you should feel good about accomplishing just one task a day. If all you get done is laundry, then that is a good day. If going to the post office or paying the electric bill took all afternoon, good! You got one thing accomplished.

Throw away your to-do list and plan on slowing things down. Due to heavy-handed bureaucracy, dependence on public transportation, limited household conveniences and struggling with a new language, getting things done just isn't the same as it is back home.

Cultures differ, plain and simple. In the U.S. we respect and highly esteem quick decision making. "He really thinks quickly on his feet" is a compliment to most North Americans. Not all cultures consider that a value. Daily life may be frustrating at first and you might feel as if all your norms and cultural cues are wrong. You'll be dealing with basic presuppositions that conflict with what you know and understand of the world.

John L., M.A., Biblical Studies, Akwanga, Nigeria

I was in Jos on a Saturday attending a special ceremony for a friend of mine. He was being installed as the new national president of a missions organization here. Just before the ceremony began, my cell phone rang. Dr. Ogga, the head of my department, asked me, "Please, can you accompany us to Zaria this coming Monday and Tuesday?" I responded, "Sure. What is the occasion?" He replied, "We need to coordinate a set of exam questions for our Bachelor of Science students there. It will be a time for rubbing of the minds." Not a lot of pre-planning goes on here.

So the day after returning from Jos, I left early in a small bus for a four-hour journey with Dr. Ogga and four other lecturers. We arrived safely and participated in several hours of meetings. When we went in search of something for supper on the campus, we were informed that the "food is finished."

Then I found out that I would be sharing a room in a very small hotel with Dr. Ogga that night. He was recovering from cataract removal/lens implant surgery, so it was up to me to administer his eye drops (four times daily) during the two days we were together. I was very tired and more than a little put out by the last night, when Dr. Ogga said to me, "My brother, I am so glad you came to help ease our workload. Your enthusiasm and energy are an inspiration to us. You are so happy and you don't complain, even though you only found out about this trip two days before we left. You like it here and like working with us even in spite of all the mayhem, bad roads, lack of electricity and all the other inconveniences. It does my heart good to have a colleague like you and your wife. You are such good examples to our students and you teach the Word of God so faithfully. Thank you for coming!"

What does one say to that kind of compliment? All I could think of was, "Thank you, brother. It is indeed a great privilege and an answer to several years of prayer to be here." I turned off the lights and we went to sleep.

- Time versus event orientation

- Right/wrong versus cultural norms

- Community versus individuality

- Doing versus being

- Direct speech versus ambiguous speech

It may be hard to function when "no" doesn't always mean no, when direct speech is considered ill-mannered and ambiguity is a part of normal discourse. What do you do when people don't respect time and schedules? How do you handle events that don't really have a beginning or an end, like church services that run all day and weddings that never quite seem to start? Simple—you learn to adapt.

This book is not an exhaustive guide to crosscultural living and adjustments. We just want to encourage you not to judge your host nation and its people. An important mantra for healthy adjustment is: "It's not good; it's not bad. It's just different."

Suggestions:

If you are teaching in a culture that differs significantly from your home culture, be aware of conflicts that may arise related to time and decision making. You ask your department head if you can take your class to a special event taking place in September. The answer is yes, but the answer doesn't come until November. Or people may ask you to do things for them that you think will be a poor use of your time. It is not that these individuals don't value your time or can't make decisions. Rather they just view things from a different perspective.

Your response should be one of learning and patience. Don't get angry and frustrated with last-minute changes in schedules or a colleague that forgets to tell you about a departmental meeting. Even if you never fully understand the whys behind all the differences, it becomes easier to deal with them.

Regarding social engagements: Try to accept as many as possible, but guard your time and your attitude as you accept invitations. It can be unwise to accept a dinner invitation and then arrive with a nega-

Olga A., Ph.D., Russian Language and Cultural Studies, Asia

Sometimes God has to work very hard to show me he has the best plan for me! When I got my schedule for second semester, I couldn't say I liked it. I was hoping to have more free time, but I was going to have a very busy semester, plus one new subject I had never taught before. Shortly after I got the new schedule, my dean called me and asked if I could teach just one more class: "Methodology of Conducting Scientific Research." I didn't want to teach it, because it too was a new subject for me and I felt this class would require a lot of preparation. I simply didn't feel able to teach it. I wanted to say "No." I was trying to do my best to explain to her why it wouldn't work, and after some wrestling I finally gave up. I can't say that I had a good attitude about this. I just knew this class would be a difficult one for me and my students.

When I met with the graduate students for the first time, I asked them about their scientific interests. I was hoping to find something in common with at least some of them. I had five students in the class, and one said that she already started to work on her dissertation. The theme was a biblical basis of Russian literature. She said she would love to know more about the Bible and asked the group if they would agree to study it in class sometimes. My reaction was probably strange to my students: I lifted up my eyes to the ceiling and murmured, "Lord, thank you for this class, for now I know why you wanted me to teach this class. And please forgive me for trying to resist and for not trusting you that you know better."

Students asked me to give a lecture about the distinctions between Christianity and other religions. Through this God provided an opportunity for me to explain what salvation is, who Christ is and why I believe the Bible. During the eighteen weeks of this class, we read the Bible, discussed it and even used it for homework. It did indeed take a lot of preparation for this class, but it was so rewarding. I was really blessed to teach it and I prayed that the Holy Spirit would touch the minds and hearts of my students.

tive attitude that reflects poorly on you and your work. The key is to be flexible and slowly make transitions into your host culture.

EXPECTATIONS ABOUT SHARING THE GOSPEL

American Christians too often get caught up in numbers used to determine ministry effectiveness. The more individuals who come to Christ, the more effective the ministry, right? We often need to slow down and realize that as outsiders we must earn the right to be heard. Our expectations may be way out of sync with what actually happens. Here are some common mistaken assumptions:

- I will be sharing my faith all the time every day because evangelism is *real* missionary work.

- Most people will be open to hearing the gospel from me because what I have to say is significant, so of course they'll listen.

- Telling others about Jesus Christ is the most important thing I can do—the only truly significant thing I do.

- Have I really accomplished anything if I haven't won others to Christ?

Reality:
Followers of Jesus are eager to introduce others to him. But are the above assumptions realistic? Sharing the gospel is a priority and requires prayer and thought. Sharing with students and colleagues takes time. Those teaching in a distant classroom must *earn the right to be heard.* That takes time, service and investing in people's lives. It usually does not come easily.

Adrian H. went to teach at Moscow State University's department of philosophy shortly after the fall of communism. Adrian was a seasoned border-crosser: born in Holland, raised in Canada, full-time missionary in the Philippines. However, Adrian was dumbfounded by the hardheartedness of his students and colleagues. No one ever seemed interested in talking about spiritual things. Building relationships seemed impossible. Adrian prayed earnestly about this, but nothing seemed to work. He struggled with discouragement.

One day the department chair announced the university had given money to remodel their 1940s-era faculty office. (In Russia professors don't have individual offices but share a large room with many desks and one secretary.) Adrian had put himself through college hanging wallpaper. It was a skill he was quite good at. So when the department chair announced there would be a workday that weekend to strip wallpaper, paint and remodel the office, Adrian quickly volunteered.

"Can you do labor, Dr. Adrian?" the department chair asked with a bit of sarcasm. "I'll do my best," Adrian replied and he showed up first thing Saturday to start the labor project. For two long days he worked alongside colleagues. Adrian stripped wallpaper, caulked holes in the wall, listened to others' stories, shared a few jokes, and with great skill and precision hung the new paper. Once the office was finished the department chair announced that they would have a party to celebrate. They set a time and everyone agreed to contribute food and vodka for the occasion. Adrian was heading home exhausted but with a sense of accomplishment when the department chair asked if he might have a word with Adrian.

"All these months we have worked together I have never wanted to know anything about you or your God. But now, seeing you work so hard and doing so much for this department, I am now ready to listen." He went on to ask Adrian, a licensed minister, "We need a priest to say a blessing over our new office. You are a kind of priest, aren't you? Would you do us the honor of praying a blessing over our new office the night of our celebration?" Adrian did. He realized earning the right to share one's faith sometimes requires a little wallpapering.

Suggestions:
It is vital to establish yourself as a good teacher, researcher, colleague and sometimes a good wallpaper-hanger before sharing the gospel. If you don't have credibility as a professor in the eyes of your students and colleagues, then you won't have credibility as a messenger for Christ. Be patient, work hard and pray for opportunities. Paul tells us in 1 Corinthians 3 that some plant, some water and some reap. Be comfortable with where you are in the process.

ADDITIONAL AREAS TO CONSIDER

Political differences. Consider what it will be like moving from a Western country where freedom of speech is held in high regard and diverse views are tolerated, even celebrated, to a highly controlled society where conformity is expected and enforced. Reflect on how you will handle knowing your phone conversations and emails may be monitored and that numerous websites are blocked because they present viewpoints considered illegal by the government.

Regardless of your home country or where you are going, leave your patriotism at home. Never wrap the gospel in the American flag. You are not there to defend your nation; you are there to live out Christ. Winning a friend is more important than winning a political argument.

Religious differences. Consider the implications of moving from your home culture where Christianity is dominant to a country where your faith is under constant surveillance and suspicion. In some countries, those who follow Christ are thought to be evil infidels.

Personal safety. You might be moving to a place where your personal security is in question. It may not be safe to take an evening stroll alone outdoors.

Health and medical issues. Your home country probably has decent medical care, and good health standards have eliminated many diseases. Now you may be going to a country where health standards are poor, health services are unfamiliar and there are frequent viral outbreaks.

Transportation concerns. You left behind your trusty Toyota only to find yourself facing unreliable, overcrowded and unsafe public transportation. Fatal traffic accidents are not uncommon. Driving in many countries can put your sanity and life at risk.

The best piece of advice is to expect the unexpected and reflect upon what is happening before reacting. If you want your students and colleagues to know the love of the Savior, let them see him in your behavior. "The LORD is compassionate and gracious, slow to anger and abounding in lovingkindness" (Ps 103:8 NASB).

GOING DEEPER, GOING FURTHER

Questions to Consider

1. What crosscultural travel or work experiences have you had? What kinds of expectations did you have beforehand, and how did they line up with reality?

2. What expectations do you have about your teaching experience? About living overseas?

3. What do you anticipate will be your biggest challenge overseas? What might be your easiest adjustment?

4. What can you do beforehand to set realistic expectations for yourself? Find resources or people that can help prepare you for on-the-ground realities of your particular context.

Suggested Reading List

Basic Concepts of Intercultural Communication: Selected Readings, edited by Milton Bennett

Do's and Don'ts Around the World: A Country Guide to Cultural and Social Taboos and Etiquette, Gladson Nwanna (1998). This includes volumes on Africa, the Caribbean, Europe, the Middle East, Japan and Russia. It's from World Travel Institute, Baltimore.

Passport to Mission, E. W. Baumgartner et al., available online at http://www.adventistvolunteers.org/Forms/Passport.pdf

Survival Kit for Overseas Living: For Americans Planning to Live and Work Abroad (4th ed.), L. Robert Kohls

REFERENCE LIST

Baumgartner, E. W., Dybdahl, J. L., Gustin, P., & Moyer, B. C. (2002). *Passport to mission* (2nd ed.). Andrews University, Berrien Springs, MI: Institute of World Mission.

Thurston, A., Turner-Gottschang, K., & Reed, L. (1994). *China bound* (2nd ed.). Washington, DC: National Academy Press.

9

Dealing with Culture Shock

I (Mike) and a male graduate student presented a workshop on web-based programs at an all-girls primary school (with an all-female faculty) in the Middle East. I presented my twenty-minute theory and practice lesson, and my grad student took over demonstrating the ins and outs of the program. During his presentation a teacher (wearing an *abaya* cloak and veil) signaled me to come and help her with a problem. I went immediately to her, stood over the computer and pointed to the keyboard attempting to help her. I solved the problem and walked away satisfied. I did a pretty good job of one-on-one teaching.

Within seconds, the school's principal approached and requested I follow her to the hallway. I thought she was going to praise me because the teachers were so engaged in our workshop. After all, I had just demonstrated some excellent individual instruction. That thought was quickly shattered when she scolded me for getting too close to the teacher. She told me the other teachers criticized my "close" interaction with her. She said, "Obviously you don't understand our culture where men are to keep a meter's distance when interacting with women."

I was hurt and embarrassed for causing such a problem, especially when I thought I did a great job. I had to go back into that room and finish the workshop. Nervous, and with a pit in my stomach, I regrouped. Afterward, when providing individual instruction, I sat at the computer and requested that the teachers come to me because they knew the appropriate distance required. Although my intentions and motives were pure, my naiveté to cultural norms disrupted the workshop and created a rather serious crosscultural conflict.

Everyone living and working overseas faces *culture shock*. What exactly is culture shock and how does it affect those living in crosscultural settings? Culture shock is an overreaction to cultural norms in a place where customs and behavior are very different from anything previously experienced. Culture shock is usually precipitated by anxiety that results from losing familiar signs and symbols of social intercourse, such as language, table manners, protocol for greeting people and what is considered humor. These provide information and security about who we are and what to do. When we lose the props that support us, cultural adjustment becomes very difficult.

Experts describe culture shock as an emotional state of stress that can become depression because of the constant exposure and interaction with people whose values, beliefs, worldviews and ways of life conflict with our own. Culture shock was first described by Oberg (1960) as being almost like a disease: it has a cause, symptoms and a cure. Oberg found that individuals can actually experience similar feelings to illness when they live in a different country or culture.

CAUSES

When we enter a strange new culture, most of our familiar cues are lost. We experience:

- Inability to read and write the host culture's language; we essentially become illiterate

- Inability to speak or understand the language; we become hearing and speaking impaired

- Unfamiliarity with the local customs and social norms
- A lack of security and/or well-being
- Difficulty completing "simple" or "normal" tasks (making a phone call, doing laundry)
- The weight and difficulty of daily living (grocery shopping, public transportation)
- Inability to "fit in" with the culture around you (e.g., as a Caucasian, I will never be Chinese)
- Changes in relationships
- Disorientation of values

SYMPTOMS

There are many symptoms of culture shock, but you don't have to have every symptom to experience it! Here are a few (Baumgartner et al., 2002):

- Feeling angry over minor inconveniences
- Unusual irritability over the local way of life
- Withdrawal from the host nationals
- Extreme homesickness
- Sudden intense feeling of loyalty to your own culture and an attitude of superiority
- Overall feeling of dissatisfaction; rising stress, distrust and depression
- A change in sleep patterns: wanting to sleep all the time or not being able to sleep
- Obsession with health, cleanliness, clean food and water; excessive hand washing

This is not a comprehensive list, but it provides some idea of the mental, physical and emotional effects of living in a distant land. The key is not trying to avoid culture shock (this is impossible anyway) but developing sound strategies to cope with the stress that accompanies living in an unfamiliar culture. The degree to which an individual suffers from culture shock can vary depending upon a variety of factors such as personality, the extent of differences between the cultures, and the way people deal with and adapt to new situations (Baumgartner et al., 2002).

CURE

Understanding the Stages of Culture Shock

The first step in recovering from culture shock is to recognize you have it. Psychologists suggest that there are four distinct stages of culture shock. All people who travel and live abroad deal with these stages to varying degrees (Pedersen, 1995).

Stage One: The Honeymoon Stage

Most people are fascinated by the new. Barring a few minor problems, the first weeks in a new country usually go smoothly. You will be excited about the adventure of being in a new place. You will be exhilarated to have finally arrived after so much preparation and anticipation. There are novel and exciting smells, food, sights and people. Even when a few problems arise, these are written off as just being part of the new experience.

You're in the honeymoon stage when:

- You love everything around you
- Everyone and everything in the new culture seems wonderful
- You are full of fascination, wonder and awe at your host culture
- Every day is an adventure and you really enjoy discovering things
- You're blind to all your host nation's imperfections
- You find so many things "charming"

However, this superficial and unrealistic experience of the culture soon fades. And you're on to stage two.

Stage Two: The Rejection Stage

Then it hits you! The little things you found charming at first now grate on your nerves. *Why don't they put their bread in bags?*

Standing in line for hours to get a registration card, a car permit or to pay your telephone bill suddenly seems like the end of the world. You begin to wonder why you came to this strange land in the first place and how long you can last. Judgmentalism sets in. You begin to think in "us" versus "them" categories. You become hostile, aggressive, frustrated and certain that the cultural norms you find so irritating are actually intentional. *They just don't understand me.*

Symptoms of this stage include:

- Excessive desire to control one's environment

- Being overly critical of the host nation; being cynical, derogatory and sarcastic toward the host culture

- A sense that nationals are unfriendly and unsympathetic

- An inability to see the host nationals as real people; a feeling of alienation and isolation

- A feeling of helplessness

- An overriding attitude of superiority toward the host nationals: *Why do they do it that way? They don't queue up. They have squat toilets. They crowd me in public and don't respect my personal space.*

This can be the "make or break" phase. The individual either gets stronger and stays or becomes weaker and decides to go home. She starts to count down the days to when her time there is over. If you read this and are tempted to think, *That won't happen to me,* trust us—you will face these issues at some point in your crosscultural experience.

Stage Three: The Colonization Stage

This stage occurs as a direct result of self-preservation. This is considered by experts as the *peak* or *crisis* of the entire process. If you come out of this stage, you are more likely to stay. If you never leave this frame of mind, chances are you'll go home before your contract or commitment is up.

Colonization happens when you just want to be with "people like you." International fellowships and churches can be an easy way to escape the host culture and hide in your own colony.

How long does this stage last? This depends on how well you use coping strategies and how aware you are that it is going on. Ignored colonization is very dangerous. It can impede effective ministry and impact your witness for Christ.

Try to avoid too much dependency on the local expatriate community. Avoid cultural ghettos where citizens from your home country gather to criticize, mock and berate the local culture. You are not there for the expat community of like-minded individuals; you are there for the nationals. The sooner you integrate into local life, the better.

Symptoms of this stage include:

- An overdependence on long-term expatriates
- Preferring the company of people from your own culture and intentionally seeking them out
- A terrible longing to be back home
- A glamorized view of home
- Constantly comparing and contrasting the host culture with an idealized view of your own nation

The person who ignores these attitudes and allows them to fester moves backward and fails to learn and gain insight from their host culture. The foreigner who spends time obsessed with trying to create the atmosphere of "home" in the new situation is defeated. In this phase you reflect upon only the good things about your home country. The negative aspects of your homeland are forgotten, and you begin to wonder why you ever left. Psychologists suggest that if an individual deals well with stage two of culture shock, they will only briefly struggle with stage three and move right to stage four.

Stage Four: The Adjustment Stage

Finally, an honest appreciation for your host culture develops. You accept the customs of the new country in a realistic and healthy way. Things are what they are. *They're not good; they're not bad. They're just different.* You may not like everything about the new culture, but you can operate within their norms.

In this adjustment stage we still have cultural stress and problems to contend with, but we become more empathetic, understanding that people are people—the good, the bad and the ugly. As we adjust, our self-confidence increases. As we interact more freely with the host culture, a new identity emerges: we find ourselves as participants in the culture and no longer just grumpy, discontent observers.

In this stage, you are about 90 percent adjusted and you begin to see the similarities of the country with your homeland. You understand that for the most part, your two countries just have different lifestyles and different ways to deal with the problems of life. The food, habits, customs—all the things you thought you would never get used to—now seem normal. You now prefer some things, maybe many things, in the new culture. You might even find yourself thinking that you will miss certain things when you go back home.

The adjustment stage doesn't mean culture shock is finished. The dreaded disease can rear its ugly head on occasion, but it means you have mostly learned to cope with the symptoms of culture shock. You have learned to adjust to your new home.

COPING WITH CULTURE SHOCK

First of all, don't disregard culture shock or the effects that it may have on you. Instead, realize that it will affect you. Learn to recognize signs of the stages. Try different strategies to cope with your particular situation and practice the ones that work for you. Here are a few more suggestions for coping with culture shock.

Be realistic. Most people experience culture shock in some way while they are overseas. Just recognize the problem and give yourself time to get over it.

• Keep reminding yourself that this is not permanent.

- Set fair and realistic expectations for yourself and for others.
- Be patient, be flexible and tolerate ambiguity.

Become informed and get involved. Don't be passive. Be intentional about learning your new culture.

- Study the language. This will not only help you feel more at home as you understand what is being said and what is happening around you, it will also help you gain credibility with others.

- Find books and websites that provide knowledge about culture shock and the host culture. This will help you understand why things are the way they are and why you are feeling as you do.

- Make friends with nationals and go to things you are invited to. Invite nationals to do things with you.

- Learn the currency, learn the mass transit system and learn how to live on local products.

Have a sense of humor. In another culture you will have many experiences that can lead to anger, annoyance, embarrassment and discouragement. Learning a new language and culture can make you feel like a child: dependent on others and always having to learn new things. Find something humorous in each situation. This helps reduce stress levels and provides you with a little more grace for those frustrating experiences. Don't laugh at the culture or its people, but feel free to laugh at yourself. Don't take yourself too seriously. Laughter also guards against despair. After all, "A cheerful heart is good medicine, but a crushed spirit dries up the bones" (Prov 17:22). Don't take things personally. This really is not all about you!

Don't forget the physical. Teaching overseas can place enormous stress on your body. Develop a steady pattern of exercise. Finding a physical activity that you enjoy will reduce stress and help keep you healthy. Exercise routines developed before you left home can be a source of comfort and familiarity when you continue in the new setting. However, don't count on going to Curves or using the Bowflex at the Y; keep it simple. Walk, run, play basketball. Also, many people find they require one to three more hours of sleep each night while living crossculturally. So get plenty of rest.

Be open-minded, flexible and adaptable. The ability to be adaptable, flexible and receptive to new stimuli is needed for intercultural adjustment because we all face unexpected situations. Learn to tolerate ambiguity and differences in your new environment. Have a sympathetic understanding for practices that differ, and keep judgmental behavior to a minimum.

Develop the ability to cope with failure. The ability to tolerate failure is important because *everyone* fails at something overseas. Become a learner. A successful overseas experience requires a great deal of learning. Ask questions. A gentle, humble attitude that asks, "Why does this work like this?" or "Can you help me understand why you made this choice?" is usually received well. You will learn from the answers you get. As you learn about other people, places, ideas and cultural traits, you will learn new ways to adapt to the new environment. Although you may not fully agree, you will at least understand better.

Develop a consistent prayer life. Your teaching, your witness and how you handle difficult situations are affected by your spiritual life. Prayer allows us to see the bigger picture, provides peace and enables God to work through us. Just as you will cultivate your relationships with the people you are serving, you must develop and cultivate your relationship with the Lord. You cannot do this without him. Anticipate obstacles that stand in the way of having a consistent devotional life overseas. Identify things that disrupt your prayer life and then remove those obstacles. Pray knowing God hears you. Then start looking for how and when he responds. Make worship a regular part of your daily life. Bring the sacrifice of praise to your devotions—when you're suffering from culture shock, it can feel like a sacrifice to praise God. A garment of praise can counteract a spirit of heaviness.

Find support and fellowship. Become active in a Christian fellowship as soon as possible. This provides support, encouragement and growth that will be sorely needed. In some cases, you may not have any sort of fellowship or place for Christians to gather. This can be especially difficult if you have not developed the daily habit of worship and intimacy with

God. Where even two or three are gathered in Jesus' name, he is in their midst (Mt 18:20). This can be a teammate or your spouse and kids.

Occasionally take time to enjoy your home culture. Experience your home culture, whether it is a McDonald's cheeseburger or an occasional cup of Starbucks coffee. Treating yourself occasionally can help ease crosscultural adjustment. If you crave McDonald's fries, find some. (Don't be too surprised if you have to pay extra for ketchup!) Watching an American movie or sitcom, eating at an American restaurant or simply enjoying something you miss from home can help deal with crosscultural frustrations.

CONCLUSION

A wise man once said, "To prepare is half the victory." You need to be well prepared before leaving to teach crossculturally. Have realistic expectations and be well informed beforehand by reading, talking with others and searching online to find information about the culture, students and life in the country where God has called you to serve.

There is nothing quite like living in a distant land. The excitement, adventure and learning experience are invaluable. And no matter how prepared you are, you will still face difficulties. We (the Romanowskis) were fairly well prepared for life in China. We knew beforehand that buildings in that part of China wouldn't have heat. We had heard stories and were expecting a home and classrooms without heat. But when winter arrived, it was so much more difficult to face than we had expected. I wasn't expecting to see my breath while I taught classes. I didn't expect to lose feeling in my fingers and toes while lecturing. But if I hadn't prepared for those living conditions, the results could have been devastating. I might have just packed up our family and gone home and missed one of the greatest blessings of our lives.

Teaching in a distant land is not going to transform your personality overnight. You will not escape who you are. The mundane day-to-day grind may not significantly improve. Living and teaching crossculturally has much to offer you, but make sure you have realistic expectations. Prepare for change.

Jesus Christ crossed the most difficult cultural border in history. He left paradise to walk among frail human beings who did not recognize him, were limited in their understanding of him, always questioned his authority and eventually turned against him. Christ has now commanded us to cross borders and "go into all the world" and teach (Mk 16:15). He can instruct us how to be good border-crossers, because he himself was the perfect border-crosser. Look to him during this time as you seek to become better equipped and better prepared to bring glory to his name in a distant classroom.

GOING DEEPER, GOING FURTHER

Questions to Consider

1. What do you think culture is? How do you define culture?

2. What is the difference between overt and covert culture? Give some examples.

3. What do you anticipate will be your biggest challenge overseas? What do you think will be your easiest adjustment?

Suggested Reading List

"Culture Shock: Negotiating Feelings in the Field," Rachel Irwin, available online at http://www.anthropologymatters.com/journal/2007-1/irwin_2007_culture.pdf

Passport to Mission, E. W. Baumgartner et al. available online at http://www.Adventistvolunteers.org/Forms/Passport.pdf

Survival Kit for Overseas Living: For Americans Planning to Live and Work Abroad (4th ed.), L. Robert Kohls

Films for Multicultural Awareness

Babette's Feast (1987) G multicultural

The Beauty Academy of Kabul (2006) PG Afghani

City of Joy (1992) PG-13 Indian/religion

The Color of Paradise (1999) G Iranian

The Gods Must Be Crazy (1980) PG African

The Gods Must Be Crazy II (1989) PG *African*
A Great Wall (1986) PG-13 *Chinese*
Hotel Rwanda (2004) R *African*
The Kite Runner (2008) R *Afghani*
Liam (2000) R *Irish/poverty*
Lifting the Fog: Intrigue in the Middle East (1994) NR
The Middle of the World (2003) NR *poverty/South American*
Monsoon Wedding (2001) PG *Indian*
Not One Less (1999) G *Chinese*
Offside (2006) G *Iranian*
Raise the Red Lantern (1991) PG *Chinese*
The Road Home (2000) G *Chinese*
Russian Ark (2002) NR *Russian*
The Sea Inside (2004) PG-13 *Hispanic*
The Teahouse of the August Moon (1956) G *Asian*
Ushpizin (2004) PG *Jewish/Israeli*

REFERENCE LIST

Baumgartner, E. W., Dybdahl, J. L., Gustin, P., & Moyer, B. C. (2002). *Passport to mission* (2nd ed.). Anderson University, Berrien Springs, MI: Institute of World Mission.

Oberg, K. (1960). Culture shock: adjustment to new cultural environments. *Practical Anthropology, 7,* 177-82.

Pedersen, P. (1995). *The five stages of culture shock: Critical incidents around the world.* Westport, CT: Greenwood Press.

10

Teaching English
as a Foreign Language

The English language has become the lingua franca of the twenty-first century (Graddol, 1997). One out of every five individuals in the world studies English as a foreign language, which makes it not only the most studied language in the world, but perhaps the most studied *subject* in the world (Swerdlow, 1999). With the global expansion of the Internet, the influence of English has only increased because it is the most prevalent language among the more than 12 billion webpages worldwide. More than 80 percent of all Internet language is English (Drori, 2005). In international academia, English is the new Latin (Bollag, 2000). As a result of the global community's need to know English, teaching English as a foreign language (EFL) has become one of the largest service industries in the world (Dovring, 1997).

Christians are a majority of the world's EFL professionals. In fact, more Christians teach EFL than any other special-interest group (McCarthy, 2000). Therefore a biblically sound, Christian worldview of EFL teaching and learning is vitally important if Christian EFL teachers are to have a truly eternal impact on students in distant classrooms. In this chapter we look at some theories about teaching EFL and develop a practical direction for teaching EFL with excellence.

This is not an EFL handbook for overseas teaching. There are plenty of those on the market. We aren't offering ideas on pronunciation exercises or explaining how to correct grammatical errors in writing. Instead we provide a lens through which to view and evaluate EFL curriculum, materials and teaching strategies that will help the Christian EFL teacher to do EFL Christianly.

A Christian worldview of EFL must first acknowledge that EFL is essentially a pedagogical endeavor. It is neither an evangelistic endeavor nor is it a church-planting endeavor (though both of these are worthwhile undertakings outside the classroom). It is a *teaching* endeavor in which the individual is contracted to do a specific job—teach English. As discussed in chapter one, we think the kingdom is better served when followers of Christ teaching overseas do what they are hired to do and do it well.

Unfortunately, Christians have traveled overseas as English teachers with little or no training. Many have the simplistic assumption that because they are native English speakers, they are qualified to teach English. As a result some Christian EFL teachers have often not taught with excellence and thus have not brought glory to God nor served the profession or their students well.

Christian EFL teachers must realize that they must intentionally develop a Christian worldview of EFL as well as acquire some teaching experience and EFL teacher education. All teaching, including EFL, begins with understanding that teaching is a calling and "a legitimate vehicle for their life" and not "just an excuse for it" (Anderson, 2001). With that in mind, let's look at some EFL materials, strategies and methods in light of Christian faith.

Consider the essay on page 182, which appeared in the introduction to *Modern English-Language Reader, Book Two*, published in 1974 by the Beijing Foreign Languages Institute to teach English reading and writing to university students. What's wrong with this essay? It is politically or philosophically sound if you're an anti-Confucius socialist. Certainly we understand that politics and philosophy are important aspects of language learning. But what about this essay hin-

An Essay to Criticize Lin Piao and Confucius

Confucius was a reactionary who doggedly defended slavery and whose doctrines have been used by all reactionaries, whether ancient or contemporary, Chinese or foreign, throughout the more than 2,000 years since his time. The bourgeois careerist, renegade and traitor Lin Piao was a thorough devotee of Confucius and, like all the reactionaries in Chinese history when on the road to their doom, he revered Confucius, opposed the Legalist School and attacked Chin Shih Huang, the first emperor of the Chin Dynasty (221-207 B.C.). He used the doctrines of Confucius and Mencius as a reactionary ideological weapon in his plot to usurp Communist Party leadership, seize state power and restore the bondage of capitalism in China.

The worker-peasant-soldier masses of China are the main force in the criticism of Lin Piao and Confucius. They plunge into the struggle with strong revolutionary indignation. It is with the aim of helping the reader to understand this campaign of criticism that we have collected these articles by workers, peasants and soldiers, reflecting their conscientious study of theory and their revolutionary spirit in using Marxism-Leninism-Mao-Ze-Dong-Thought as a weapon, integrating theory with practice and overcoming every difficulty on their way to learning. The articles also show that a theoretical force of the Chinese workers, peasants and soldiers has been formed and is steadily growing in the struggles of the Great Proletarian Cultural Revolution and the criticism of Lin Piao and Confucius.

ders *real, authentic* English language learning? Are they using correct verb forms? Are the pronouns agreeing with the nouns? Is the basic structure "standard" English? Yes. All of these important aspects of EFL reading and writing are presented well. The problem is that the worldview being conveyed in this essay is not representative of the worldview of *most* English-speaking nations.

The question must be considered: "Is the *language* in this essay authentic?" No, it is not. Countries that speak English as their national language don't normally use the kind of vocabulary found in "An Essay to Criticize." It's not a part of the average Joe's or Jane's water-cooler conversation. It lacks the tone of an authentic English-language essay because the vocabulary is not that of a genuine native-English speaker living in an English-speaking country. However, it expresses the values, ideals, ethics, principles and history the Chinese government wanted its students to believe as true. And it demonstrates that *language teaching is never without a message, never without a worldview and never value-free.*

RUNNING WITH THE BIG DOGS

Moravian scholar John Amos Comenius (1592-1671) developed a Christian worldview of teaching foreign language. Foreign languages were an intrinsic part of education in his time, especially Latin (Panek, 1991). In what is considered to be his greatest work, *The Great Didactic*, published in 1642, Comenius wrote, "Languages are learned, not as forming in themselves a part of erudition or wisdom, but as being the means by which we may acquire knowledge and may impart it to others . . . for it is men we are preparing, not parrots" (Comenious/Keatinge trans., 1910/1967, p. 203). Notice the far-reaching perspective put forth in Comenius's statement. It moves us beyond grammar and sentence structure to seeing our students—the language learners—as human.

Above all, the Christian teacher heading overseas to teach EFL must be committed to the principle that he is teaching human beings and not just training parrots to reproduce meaningless English phrases and expressions. In the same vein as Comenius, David Smith (2007), challenges foreign language teachers to ask the question, "How would I *teach* differently if I believed that my students were spiritual beings?" (p. 41). In other words, "How would I teach if I truly see my students as whole persons needing whole language in a whole context?" Smith writes that we are "starting, after all, from the premise that they are not machines, not docile information-processing mechanisms, but living images, shaping, misshaping and reshaping themselves" (p. 47). Although that may sound elementary, it is a powerful insight and a vital truth for Christian EFL teachers who want to impact their students for Christ. That difference may seem obvious, but in fact some EFL classroom techniques become a simple exercise in repeating mindless phrases and irrelevant language patterns. Teaching EFL Christianly means teaching students how to think in the English language. It means imparting the skills necessary for them to speak real language originating from the speaker, from the speaker's heart and mind.

Comenius's approach to language learning was revolutionary for its time. In 1631, Comenius wrote his definitive work on foreign language teaching, *The Gate of Languages,* a textbook for the introduction of teaching Latin in accordance with his philosophy of education. He desired to move foreign language from a rote memorization methodology (still practiced today in countries where EFL is mandatory in public schools) into a new realm of practical and useful understanding. "Comenious [sic] saw the teaching of language as particularly problematic and argued that methods of rote memory and recitation should be abandoned in favor of more natural means" (Lochman, as cited in Comenius/Louthan & Sterk, 1623/1998, p. 18).

Comenius "rescued the boys of his generation from the sterile study of words and introduced them to the world of mechanics, politics, and morality" (Comenius/Keatinge, 1910/1967, p. 24). He made foreign language learning useful and practical. Comenius encouraged students to see the beauty of language and not just its function. Not understanding the deeper purposes of EFL will result in a teacher's inability to see the beauty of language and will demean EFL teaching to that of mere function.

It is not our purpose in this chapter to present a comprehensive analysis of Comenius's methods and pedagogical theories. But we do want to illustrate, through the example of Comenius, that as a Christian his method of language learning and teaching transformed the past and even current educational communities. In fact, his approach to foreign language education was so sound and user-friendly that even those who strongly opposed his Reformed theology could not deny the effectiveness of his teaching strategies and adopted his foreign language teaching techniques. Amazingly, at the very time when Jesuit priests were demanding Comenius's death for heresy, they were using his textbook and teaching approaches in every Jesuit school in Europe.

The Gate of Languages was still being used well into the 1800s, long after Comenius's death:

> Seldom in the history of language teaching has it been so closely related to the personal and social environment of the learner as it was in these new texts, which probably explains their survival more than three centuries after their creation and their continued use in certain parts of Europe even at the present time. (Murphy, 1995, p. 195)

His revolutionary approach to language learning introduced performing plays in the target language, journaling, oral book reports and the idea that learning could be fun and enjoyable (Murphy, 1995). He formed and articulated a Christian worldview of foreign language learning that transformed the educational community of his time.

Another great Christian scholar who allowed his faith to inform his view of languages is Wycliffe Bible translator and world-renowned linguist Kenneth Lee Pike (1912-2000). After being rejected by a missionary society for service to China in 1933, Pike became interested in the study of language. Pike received his Ph.D. in linguistics from the University of Michigan where he served as a professor from 1955 to 1977. He was nominated for the Nobel Peace Prize fifteen years straight as a result of his work in linguistics (though never awarded). Pike's theory of the relationship between human behavior and language—*tagmemics*—is recognized as one of the greatest contributions to linguistics of the twentieth century (Switchenberg, 2006). (To learn more about Pike's tagmemics theory go to www.sil.org.)

This well-respected scholar who lived and worked among language groups in nearly a dozen nations once wrote, "I am a Christian who believes that Christ is the embodiment of truth, and that His words are therefore truth. Christ furthermore, claimed that truth came through human language" (as cited in Brend, 1972, p. 303). Pike (1958) describes Christ as "the whole context of our lives—He who Himself is the whole, linguistic 'A to Z'" (p. 262). Pike believed "Language is in the creative image of God. . . . If language is reflecting deeply the image of God, do not expect it to be simple, now or ever—nor for any theory to exhaust it" (Brend, pp. 308-9).

John Robbins (Clark, 1993), in his introduction to *Language and Theology*, echoes Pike's belief that "not only is language completely adequate and, properly used, meaningful, but its origin is God himself" (p. vi). Perhaps this is what is meant by John 1:1, "In the beginning was the Word." EFL teachers must see that language is not *just* a subject to be studied or taught. It is not a means to an end, but as Robbins and Pike argued, language has its very origin in God and is created by him for him.

Pike (1972) proposed that "language directs and guides" (as cited in Brend, p. 311) and that language should be used to help people express their personalities. "Language identifies person. Language identifies us. . . . Language concentrates life's memories, truths and joys. It expresses them, and guides them, and concentrates them. . . . Words are like that . . . they concentrate truth and joys" (pp. 309-10).

When teaching English as a foreign language, the EFL teacher should recognize and understand that teaching Christianly starts by seeing language from this perspective: People, who are created in the image of God, are being taught how to use language, which according to Pike, is also created in the image of God. EFL teachers must recognize that their purpose is to show students how to convey "truth and joy," feelings, emotions and *ideas* in the English language. And in some cases, this English language being taught may be the very tool God uses to reveal his only Son to the student for the very first time.

Here is how it can happen. In conversation with the EFL teacher or in the context of discussing a literature metaphor drawn from the Bible, the EFL student may hear for the first time in his life that Jesus is the Son of God. At that moment the English language becomes a holy instrument used by God to draw this student to himself. EFL teachers must understand the significance of teaching language and not fall into the trap Smith (2007) calls the "mind-body dichotomy" (p. 38). Smith explains: "It means combining the processes of language learning with matters such as ethics, hospitality, failure, the nature of the good life, questions of value and the source of hope, responses to human need, cross-generational interaction" (p. 46).

For example, my (Teri's) Chinese graduate students wanted to perform the Christmas story for the university. They asked me to write it as a play. I chose the Gospel of Luke and wrote a part for each student in the class. One day during rehearsal, in front of the entire class, the herald angel, Mr. Wu, announced that he believed in Jesus Christ as his Savior! This was during a time when the government was cracking down on "spiritual pollution" such as Christianity, democracy and human rights. I was stunned by his bold proclamation. Students were shocked. Some even laughed out of nervousness. Not knowing quite what to do, I asked, "Why do you say that, Mr. Wu?"

He answered, "Well, I was thinking about the words I say in the play, 'Fear not, for behold I bring you good tidings of great joy which will be for all people. For unto you this day in the city of Bethlehem a child is born, a Savior who is called Christ the Lord. Glory to God in the highest and on earth peace and goodwill toward all men.'

"I like those words and they made me feel something. So, I decided that I would receive the baby Jesus as a Savior and when I did, his peace came to me. My wife did this also."

It was a play, a tool to help EFL students learn English. Mr. Wu had only three lines, and those three lines forever changed his life.

Christian scholar C. S. Lewis also helps us understand the significance of language teaching. Lewis's *The Abolition of Man* (1944/1996) was written in response to his frustrations with the content of English textbooks in the U.K. Here Lewis warned teachers of English not to create "men without chests." In other words, do not create students lacking in a value system and without the ability to differentiate between right and wrong. Lewis's point is that even in teaching English, good values must be conveyed. "It is the doctrine of objective value, the belief that certain attitudes are really true and others really false, to the kind of thing the universe is and the kind of things we are" (p. 31). Lewis understood the power of language and the significance of language teaching. He exposed the errors of relativism in an English textbook. He eloquently explained that words and language have consequences, and that English teaching is a grave responsibility because language influences the way students see the world:

> The very power of Gaius and Titius [the authors/teachers] depends on the fact that they are dealing with a boy: a boy who thinks he is "doing" his "English prep" and has no notion that ethics, theology, and politics are all at stake. (Lewis, 1944/1996, p. 20)

Lewis's challenge to *all* educators, which is specifically appropriate for EFL teachers, is to *think* about *what* they are teaching. Values are transferred in the classroom from curriculum to student, from teacher to student, and from student to student. If there truly is a cause and effect between ideas and languages, then languages cannot be taught without ideas (Grenz, 2000). A comprehensive Christian worldview of EFL understands that language curriculum and materials are relevant, because values and ideas are conveyed through these means.

EVALUATING EFL CURRICULUM

In keeping with Lewis's ideas, we need to pose three questions (Smith & Carvill, 2000) when we look at EFL curriculum and the materials we select for teaching English overseas:

1. What values are being taught here?

2. What values are missing in this curriculum?

3. Is authentic language emphasized in these lessons?

It's not the clear-cut, brazen worldview examples that we saw in the opening of this chapter that are the real problems. Those things are more easily seen and can be dealt with directly (see our discussion of hidden curriculum in chapter four). It is the more hidden things, things that are said more subtly and perhaps without our notice on first glance—the buried and subliminal messages—that need to be examined.

That is why we must carefully evaluate language learning texts. EFL textbooks are often filled with images of beautiful people doing beautiful things at beautiful locations. Language is more than consumer-obsessed hobbies and mindless conversations. Language is more than participating in commerce, going on vacations, eating or going to a movie (Smith, 2007). These are legitimate language scenarios, but when they are the *entire* language lesson, they cheat learners of the opportunity to learn about significant issues and significant ways of communicating in the target language.

As EFL teachers we need to be aware of and challenge stereotypes written into EFL textbooks or materials. Teachers need to analyze conversations and dialogues given as illustrations of the English language to see what the curriculum believes is true about people who are native English speakers (Smith, 2007). It is here that the learner is told, "This is what people who speak English are like: they are obsessed with shopping, eating out and spending money. They do not respect the elderly, they like astrology, they are promiscuous." The curriculum tells the language learner that English-speaking communities are uniformly self-centered and oblivious to what is happening in the rest of the world.

Even worse, the hidden curriculum encourages these same kinds of attitudes and behaviors to be adopted by the learner as a new speaker of English. "If you want to be like English-speakers, you need to be promiscuous, self-centered and materialistic." This type of text projects certain behaviors, interests and attitudes for learners of the language. Through the things it asks them to do, say, see, hear and think about, it "encourages learners to talk about *this* and not *that*, to see *this* and not *that* as important, to picture themselves engaged in *this* future action and not *that*. *This*, each text suggests, is what people who are learning to speak this language are like" (Smith, 2007, p. 39)—or worse, *should* be like. As we saw in Teri's example of prepackaged curriculum in chapter four, EFL learners could easily infer from the materials that citizens of the U.S. respond negatively to the elderly and that lying is acceptable behavior.

Prepackaged EFL series are tempting because they are an "all-in-one" curriculum addressing basic EFL skills: speaking, listening, reading and writing. The instructor is provided with a workbook, a teacher's manual, DVDs and CDs—a package designed so that all the EFL teacher has to do is be a native speaker and show up. These materials are convenient and may be required by the school or program with which the teacher is working. We are challenging the Christian EFL teacher not necessarily to abandon those materials, but to teach them with eyes wide open.

We have seen firsthand curricula using atypical language scenarios to teach an objective. For example, the first lesson might be to teach the student how to give information like name, address and phone number. This is very useful language learning. However, lesson one's examples are a man being arrested telling the police officer his name, address and telephone number, and a guy at a bus stop asking a young woman, "What's your name? Can I have your telephone number?" And she gives it to him. These may seem trivial, but they speak volumes about the native English-speakers' culture to the EFL learner coming from a more traditional, conservative or religious society.

So evaluate the materials you are using. If they communicate inappropriate themes or stereotypes but you are required to use them anyway, then explain to the students through supplemental materials and your instruction that these are not norms and why you feel they are wrong. In this way you can take a bad situation and turn it for good.

Look for supplemental materials with real-life examples of people cleaning up neighborhoods (environment), working at soup kitchens (giving back) or a Habitat for Humanity project (serving others). The reality is people suffer. They die. They mourn. They make moral choices. They experience injustice. They pray. They worship. They argue. They sacrifice. They hope. They love. And, yes, they also hate (Smith, 2007). We as EFL teachers cannot and must not marginalize language.

We must be intentional about incorporating real language in real contexts so that students learn to speak authentically. When Teri studied Chinese in China, the agenda promoted by both her teacher and the text prevented her from learning Chinese vocabulary that would allow her to express her love for God and her belief in Christ. It just wasn't permitted. To this day she can order train tickets, greet fellow passengers and hold lengthy conversations with native speakers, but she is unable to share in the Chinese language the truth of Jesus Christ and the impact he has had on her life. This is the most important aspect of her personality and she cannot express it in her second language.

Here are some things to consider when previewing prepackaged materials or preparing for an EFL class:

1. Judging by the content and approach of the textbook and its stated aims, what does it seem to promote? How many of the exercises encourage learners to be good citizens and to respond to injustice? Do the people, examples and ideas presented resonate with your idea of how the world should be?

2. How is the material arranged? For example, does the text show a divide between rich/poor, work/leisure, haves/have nots and sacred/secular?

3. How does the text present people? Are women silly? Is there promiscuity? Do they appear as real human beings? Do they know

how to relate well to others? Are they polite? Are they good listeners?

4. What is the range of human tasks (such as work, vocations and callings) portrayed in the course materials? Which are missing? Are people jobless? Or do they represent a whole spectrum of vocations: doctors, janitors, preachers, teachers, students, grocery store clerks and accountants? It is good to have a broad range of citizenry that fairly represents those who speak English as their native language.

5. What is the range and quality of human relationships among the people portrayed? Is there an ethical dimension of communication? Or are human interactions superficial and meaningless? For example, do people of different generations or different ethnic backgrounds relate to one another in the text?

6. Do the people portrayed in the exercises face significant decisions involving more than just issues of personal preference or personal gain? How do they approach those decisions, and by what criteria do they make them? (For example, how to respond when the cashier gives back too much change at the market, or how to say no to someone who asks you to participate in an activity that is against your religion or personal values.)

7. Do the teaching materials include any spiritual or religious dimension in English? Or in individuals who speak it? How does the text treat this dimension—negatively or positively?

8. Do the instructional materials pay attention to marginalized members of English-speaking cultures? Do they incorporate any regrets or admitted mistakes of that culture (e.g., slavery, colonization, mistreatment of indigenous or native peoples)?

9. What does the text invite us to learn from the English speakers it presents to us? Which of their stories are we asked to listen to? What do they celebrate? What do they feel?

10. How does the text treat the learner? Does it give opportunity for open-ended and personally invested responses to issues raised? To which of the learner's interests and motives does it appeal? To which should it appeal (Smith & Carvill, 2000)?

Smith (2007) reminds us, "Obviously, no course materials are perfect, but identifying their weaknesses is necessary if we are to point those weaknesses out to our students and discuss them. It can also show us in what ways we may need to modify or supplement our instructional materials if we, as Christian educators, want them to serve our purposes" (pp.144-45).

Richard W., M.A., TEFL, Japan

One of my former students had some emotional instability that was more hidden than I realized. It didn't turn out so well. Takashi was in my class for one semester as a freshman and another semester as a sophomore. We had talked a few times about the gospel. He had visited our church and our home, and we were planning to get together at our home in the fall. Unfortunately, I never heard from Takashi in the fall. A student told me that Takashi had taken his own life.

Takashi had left a message on an online community in Japanese. He had apparently been overworked by his company, doing an internship before the end of his senior year—very difficult, with great time demands by the company—while still trying to complete his final thesis for his English literature degree. The news of Takashi's death was kept very quiet. I had thought that depression and suicide were low at Sophia University compared to the national average, but recently a Japanese teacher told me otherwise. Again, it's well hidden, but according to Jun-sensei there is widespread student depression on this campus. We pray that in the coming months and years we can be more effective in leading more students to the hope of salvation and a walk with Christ.

Be intentional. Be prayerful and thoughtful in an attempt to connect everyday processes of teaching and learning with the idea that your students are spiritual, eternal beings. Again, ask yourself, "How would I teach differently if I believed that my students were spiritual beings?"

Remember, it's not just about linguistics. We should be concerned with the whole person and how she conveys her thoughts, emotions, desires and burdens in the English language.

For too long, Christian teachers of EFL have failed to see the significance of their field. They have neglected the importance of wrestling with and developing a Christian perspective of EFL teaching materials, curriculum and methods. You want your students to walk away from your class still chewing on something, still grappling with whole-life context of language—the moral, the ethical, the significant—not just memorizing verb conjugations and new vocabulary. Your students are whole persons, body, soul, mind and heart, and your job is to teach these whole persons. And what is a more appropriate platform to do this than language?

EXAMINING TEACHING METHODS
AND STRATEGIES THROUGH A CHRISTIAN LENS

Of equal importance as curriculum is teaching strategy. Here we will look at a few of the most popular and most used methods in the EFL world today. These too need to be viewed through the lens of a Christian worldview. Table 6 summarizes the focus, problems and benefits of the three leading EFL teaching methods.

The *Grammar Translation Method* is the dirty little secret of many foreign language departments around the world. EFL trainers in the West adamantly believe this method is no longer in use, but it is. It used to be called the *Classical Method*. It was used to teach students dead languages like Latin. It focuses on grammatical rules and sentence structure, along with memorization of vocabulary lists, and encourages memorizing whole English dictionaries. It is based on rote drills and translation of literary texts. There is no provision for speaking the English language; no tools for oral communication. It is

Table 6. EFL Methods

Method/Approach	Focus	Problems	Benefits
Grammar Translation Method	Grammatical rules; sentence structure; rote/memorization; vocabulary lists; translation of texts	No provision for speaking the target language; no tools for oral communication; no student-generated language involved	Rote/memorization drills are good for irregular aspects of target language (irregular verbs, oddities of spelling, gender pronouns)
The Communicative Approach	The nature of language and the nature of the language learner; pragmatic, functional and practical applications of language; get students talking; allow students to manage their own learning; instructor is only a facilitator	Views fluency and accuracy as complementary principles underpinning communicative techniques; instructor is not to focus on student errors; not enough attention to the details of communication	Gets students talking, gives them freedom to make mistakes; gives some real-life situations for students to practice the language
Humanistic Approaches *Total Physical Response (TPR), Suggestopedia, The Silent Way, Community Learning*	Improve students' self-esteem; aim for self-actualization; teacher is not the expert; teacher is a participant; instructor does not correct errors or impose expectations	This non-corrective approach does more harm than good to the EFL learner; bad language habits are formed; there is no standard for language	Classroom is a safe place to practice English; fun exercises to get students speaking in the target language quickly

still used today for two primary reasons: comprehensive national English exams (CET Band 2 and Band 4 in China, for example) and because a few national EFL teachers can't really speak English, so it's best to keep the students' noses in the text.

The problem with the Grammar Translation Method when examined through a Christian worldview lens is this: it has no focus on real language but treats language as a cadaver. Students dissect sentences and language structures into nouns, adjectives and prepositions and learn nothing to enhance communication skills. This would be the "training parrots" Comenius mentioned. Although rote learning and memorization are a part of EFL learning, in this method they are the dominant teaching strategies. Of course these are necessary when learning irregular verbs, new vocabulary or spelling oddities, but to use this type of method exclusively is counter to everything about human expression we've discussed in this chapter.

Next, the *Communicative Approach* is touted by its supporters as not a "method" but an "approach" to language learning. Its focus is on the components of communicative competence, not just grammatical or linguistic competence. It views fluency and accuracy as complementary principles underpinning communicative techniques. In other words, get students to speak and they'll correct themselves naturally. According to Smith (1993), this approach "does not consist of the reproduction of ideal structures, but is shaped by . . . needs and attitudes" (p. 30).

Pike's (Brend, 1972) fear was that this type of language learning ignores or marginalizes the human being's personality and her emotions, which runs counter to an EFL Christian perspective because it lacks the wholeness and context of language. Furthermore, in reality few language learners, especially adults, are going to learn accuracy of verb agreement, he/she pronouns (something the Chinese struggle with immensely), and correct pronunciation just by speaking. They need correction and coaching. This approach is good in that it gets students talking, and it gives them a safe place to practice their English-speaking skills. But it focuses too much on the pragmatic and not enough on the fine-tuning of students' skills in the target language.

Finally, several *humanistic approaches* place students' self-esteem and self-concept at the center of teaching. These non-corrective approaches are aimed at getting the speaker to use the target language as quickly as possible with little concern or emphasis on accuracy (truly a deconstructionist view of teaching). The problem is that students are left to make mistakes that can and do become habitual and profoundly hinder communication. Studies have shown that this non-corrective approach does more harm than good to the EFL learner (Angle & Knight, 1998). Certainly correction must aim to help and not harm the student's spirit, but the instructor owes it to the student to enable her to be the best speaker of English she possibly can be. From a Christian perspective there are absolute truths about life, reality and language. Students of EFL need to learn the absolutes of English language and its structure—there are right and wrong ways of speaking and writing. A Christian worldview of EFL holds to these absolutes.

Christian EFL professionals desiring to live out a Christian worldview in this discipline must see that their lives, their vocations and their callings are to bring glory to God in all that they do—lesson planning, choosing materials and teaching. Teaching English as a foreign language, if done well, can help advance the kingdom of God.

GETTING EQUIPPED TO GO

EFL teachers need to learn all they can about their profession before they go. If you can't get a master's degree in EFL, then at least get certified. There are several good programs available in which non-traditional students can learn and gain principles of EFL. Go to a local community college and audit their ESL classes. Observing how it is done can help you get ideas and exposure to EFL. Read books on the subject. Search the Internet for EFL sites; there are literally thousands out there.

If your prepackaged materials are inadequate, supplement. If you know you will be teaching EFL with a prepackaged curriculum, start collecting supplemental materials from home before you leave for overseas. Cut out articles from *Reader's Digest* (it is written on an eighth-grade level) that convey ideals and principles you want your students to grapple with. Use these as reading exercises and for discussion in class (real-life language dealing with real-life issues). Find hero stories, stories of survival, stories of corruption or even the "stupid criminals" sections—all are great resource materials for introducing your students to real-life scenarios which will in turn instigate real-life language and thought.

In addition, record things and take them with you. For example, a USAir pilot was interviewed about how he saved 155 lives by landing his damaged plane in the Hudson River. Download that interview from the Internet and play it for your students. Ask questions like "Could you have remained as calm as the pilot?" "If you were a passenger on this flight, what would have been your thoughts? reactions?" "Do you think the captain is a hero?" "Are there any heroes in your life?" Have them write about it.

Record programs like NBC's *20/20* feature "What Would You Do?" This program shows people unknowingly being filmed in dilemma-based situations: Do I let that stranger leave the park with that little girl? Do I stop a drunk woman from driving? Do I tell my best friend her fiancé is already married? These types of programs stir up emotions and passions and help students convey what they think and what they would do. It is a great antidote for the artificial dialogues and scenarios often given in EFL texts. These kinds of supplemental materials engage students' listening skills and speaking skills. When you ask them to respond to a case study or a recorded show by writing, it engages their writing skills and their reading skills. But most importantly these materials engage the human brain and help students think in the target language.

Smith, a professor of German, has his students listen to a recording of an elderly woman (a German speaker) who lived through World War II. After listening to her native-German reflections, students must respond to what they have heard. Some of what she says is emotional, even heartrending. Students discuss, "If I were in that situation . . ."

and dialogue about it. They write about their thoughts on what she has shared. Have your students write stories in English about an elderly person in their lives that they value, love and appreciate. Have them interview a grandparent, an uncle, a neighbor or even the elderly janitor on campus who may often feel neglected. These exercises show your students that people and their stories matter. They illustrate the "who" of language as well as the "what" of language.

Teri has used classroom debates to engage students' heart, mind and soul. Students in countries where she has taught aren't usually permitted to express an opinion in public—a skill she feels necessary for learning English. She allows the students to pick their debate partner and then sets them up with "hot topics" that don't have specifically political or governmental overtones: things like spanking children, tattoos are good/bad, married couples should share the housework when both are employed full time, the environment is everyone's responsibility, and raising boys is easier than raising girls (or vice versa). Obesity in children, health issues, nutrition, smoking versus nonsmoking, drinking and driving, cloning—all of these are topics students usually feel passionate about and have strong opinions about but that don't get them in trouble with the powers that be. Have them engage in real topics. Sometimes it is important to avoid minefields like women's rights in Muslim nations, freedom of speech in communist countries or tolerance of minority groups in India, but find ways to get your students thinking about real-world ideas and talking in real-life language.

If possible bring films that convey the principles and values you believe are worth teaching (see list at the end of this chapter).

It's easy just to grab a set of approved prepackaged materials and let the book lay out your lesson plan and let the teacher's manual tell you what to do and when to do it. That's the easy way out. But if you want to have a real impact on your students and you want to represent a Christian worldview of EFL teaching, we believe you must evaluate what you are teaching, why you are teaching it, and how your lessons will influence your students for the rest of their lives.

GOING DEEPER, GOING FURTHER

Suggested Readings and helpful websites

Books

Engaging the Culture: Christians at Work in Education, edited by Richard Edlin and Jill Ireland

The Gift of the Stranger: Faith, Hospitality and Foreign Language Learning, David Smith and Barbara Carvill

More than a Native Speaker, Don Snow

The Spirit of the Foreign Languages Classroom, David Smith

Spiritual, Moral, Social and Cultural Education: Exploring Values in the Curriculum, edited by Stephen Bigger and Erica Brown

Spirituality, Justice and Pedagogy, edited by David Smith, John Shortt and John Sullivan

Spirituality, Social Justice and Language Learning, edited by David Smith and Terry Osborn

Teaching English as Christian Mission, Don Snow

Articles by David Smith

"Communication and Integrity: Moral Development and Modern Languages," *Language Learning Journal* 15 (1997)

"Editorial: Reflections on Authenticity," *Journal of Christianity and Foreign Languages* 3 (2002)

"Faith and Method in Foreign Language Pedagogy," *Journal of Christianity and Foreign Languages* 1 (2000)

"Gates Unlocked and Gardens of Delight: Comenius on Piety, Persons and Language Learning," *Christian Scholar's Review* 30, no. 2 (2000)

"In Search of the Whole Person: Critical Reflections on Community Language Learning," *Journal of Research on Christian Education* 6, no. 2 (1997)

Websites for Information About TESOL Certification

www.tesolcourse.com

www.teflonline.com

www.americantesol.com

www.cambridgeesol.org

A Top Ten Movie List

Choose films appropriate for your audience. Prescreen for language, sexual content and violence. Here is a list of Teri's favorites for an EFL classroom. (Also check out the movie list at the end of chapter nine.)

Amazing Grace (William Wilberforce's story)

Chariots of Fire

The Elephant Man

Groundhog Day

The Lord of the Rings trilogy

Mr. Mom

My Big Fat Greek Wedding

Spanglish

12 Angry Men (the old one with Henry Fonda)

What About Bob?

REFERENCE LIST

Anderson, P. (2001). Is tentmaking dishonest? *World Christian, 14,* 23-24.

Angle, D., & Knight, K. W. (1998, November). Debate: Should we correct students' grammar all the time, every time? *NEA Today.* [On-line] Available: http://findarticles.com/p/articles/mi_qa3617/is_199811/ai_n8819014

Bollag, B. (2000, September 8). The new Latin: English dominates in academe. *The Chronicle of Higher Education, 47*(2), A73-A76.

Brend, R. M. (Ed.). (1972). *Kenneth L. Pike selected writings.* The Hague: Mouton.

Clark, G. H. (1993). *Language and theology* (2nd ed.). Jefferson, MD: Trinity Foundation.

Comenius, J. (1967). *The great didactic.* (M. W. Keatinge, Trans.). Kila, MT: Kessinger. (Original translated work published 1910).

Comenius, J. (1998). *The labyrinth of the world & the paradise of the heart.* (H. Louthan & A. Sterk, Trans.). Mahwah, NJ: Paulist Press. (Original work published 1623).

Dovring, K. (1997). *English as lingua franca: Double talk in global per-suasion*. West Port, CT: Praeger.

Drori, G. S. (2005). *Global e-litism: Digital technology, social inequal-ity, and transnationality*. New York: Macmillan.

Graddol, D. (1997). Can English survive the new technologies? *The English Company (UK) Ltd*. [On-line], Available: www.english.co.uk/docs/iatef.htm

Grenz, S. J. (2000). What does Hollywood have to do with Wheaton? The place of (pop) culture in theological reflection. *Journal of the Evangelical Theological Society, 43*(2), 303-14.

Lewis, C. S. (1996). *The abolition of man*. (5th ed.). New York: Touch-stone. (Original work published 1944).

McCarthy, T. (2000). A call to arms: Forming a Christian worldview of teaching English as a second language. *Evangelical Missions Quarterly, 36*(3), 310-16.

Murphy, D. (1995). *Comenius: A critical reassessment of his life and work*. Portland, OR: Irish Academy Press.

Panek, J. (1991). *Jon Amos Comenius, teacher of nations*. Prague: Orbis Publishing.

Pike, K. L. (1958). *Language and life*. Dallas: Summer Institute of Linguistics.

Smith, D. (1993). Can modern language teaching be Christian? *Spec-trum, 25*(1), 25-38.

Smith, D. (2007). On viewing learners as spiritual beings: Implica-tions for language educators. *Journal of Christianity and Foreign Languages, 8*, 34-38.

Smith, D., & Carvill, B. (2000) *The gift of the stranger: Faith, hospital-ity, and foreign language learning*. Grand Rapids: Eerdmans.

Swerdlow, J. L. (1999, August). Global culture. *National Geographic Journal, 196*(2), 2-11.

Switchenberg, H. (2006). *Kenneth Lee Pike*. Minnesota State Univer-sity, Mankato E-museum [On-line], Available: www.mnsu.edu/emuseum/information/biography/pqrst/pike_kenneth_lee.html

Conclusion

Hope for the Crossing

What is the greatest crime in the desert?
Finding water and keeping silent.

ARAB PROVERB

There are 1.9 billion people on the planet right now who have never heard the name of Jesus (U.S. Center for World Mission). They didn't reject him. They didn't choose another god over him. They simply have never heard of him. These are called the unreached people of our world. Each one has a name, and that name is known to God. In fact, he has their names written on the palms of his hands and knows the hair on each of their heads (Is 49:16; Lk 12:7).

These 1.9 billion are three out of every ten people in the world. Three out of ten who will be born, live their lives, get married, have children, work jobs and navigate their entire lives without ever knowing there is a Redeemer or ever experiencing the peace of God that passes all understanding. There is no church in their community; there are no Scriptures in their language. They have never met a follower of Jesus Christ.

For some reason known only to him, God has invited us to participate with him in sharing his love, joy, hope and salvation with those around the globe who have never heard his Son's name. That's what you are doing as a teacher in a distant classroom. By deciding to leave home, comforts and all that is familiar to teach overseas, you are offering a cold cup of water in Jesus' name.

We hope that the Lord has encouraged you and directed you while reading this book. After the chalk dust settles, the classroom door is closed and the grades are recorded, your impact on your students is all that truly remains. It is our desire that as you go you will grasp the significance of your obedience to teach in a distant classroom.

Today these 1.9 billion unreached live in nations where political, religious and cultural borders are closed to traditional missions strategies. They need and want you to come as engineering professors, law and business instructors, EFL teachers. And in post-Christian nations where people are left believing in nothing, void of any faith and deceived that Christianity doesn't work—they need you too. They need you to come and teach among them and live out Christ incarnationally in their ranks. You're going not as a secret agent missionary, not as a dichotomized schizophrenic tentmaker, not as one with a hidden agenda waiting to manipulate every conversation and take your listeners hostage (metaphorically speaking, of course). You are going to live among them loving, serving, teaching, praying and living an authentic life so that the fragrance of Christ is so powerful and beautiful that they are drawn to you and therefore drawn to him. God has blessed you with a good education, lots of opportunities and the incredible gift of living in a nation where you heard the gospel freely. You are living Christ's words: "Freely you have received, freely give" (Mt 10:8).

We hope this book has challenged you to think about your motives for going overseas as a teacher. We hope you have begun to develop a Christian worldview and educational philosophy. We tossed at you as many practical tips as we possibly could and have done our best to prepare you regarding expectations and realities of overseas living. In all of that, woven throughout each chapter, we have shared with you our own experiences and the stories of others who have said yes to this amazing call to teach in distant lands.

Keep in mind that God is preparing the hearts of the individuals that will enter your classroom. Ephesians 2:10 says, "For we are what he has made us, created in Christ Jesus for good works, which God prepared beforehand to be our way of life" (NRSV). As you go on this way of life to teach overseas, remember God knows the wonderful stories he has already planned for you. In closing we each wanted to share with you a story of one of our students. Not our favorites, because good teachers don't have favorites, but good examples of what can happen when we go.

MIKE'S STORY

Faith, a thirty-year-old graduate student, read a poster inviting students to apply for a teaching assistantship for an American professor coming to her Chinese university. She had little confidence she would be selected, but she decided to apply. After a rather rigorous process, she was selected from twenty-two other candidates to serve as my teaching assistant for the year.

Faith told me later that she thought an American professor would probably be arrogant, demanding and difficult to work for. She thought his wife would be a "model type," looking down her nose at Faith and most likely rude. She was worried about the four children because she thought that American children would be mean to her, not like her and be critical of her country. On our arrival, Faith and others from the university met us at the train station and our journey together began. She was surprised that the "arrogant American professor" helped the men at the station load luggage onto a truck. She was shocked by the kids helping load stuff and how they thanked her again and again for her help.

As the year went, Faith spent hours teaching us how to adapt to Chinese culture. She was like a mother hen to the kids. Often after class she would ask me if she could come over and see them, just to spend time with them. The children loved her and treated her like family. I remember tears in Faith's eyes one evening as our five-year-old hugged her goodnight. She was amazed at our family's care for one another and our love for her and the Chinese people.

At this point in her life, she was considering joining the Communist Party in order to secure work and maybe to fill some of the void in her life. Faith was full of questions. A *lot* of questions. Many centered on our family. She asked my wife, "Why are your children so polite, obedient and loving?" My wife explained that we tried using God's plan for raising children and we prayed over them a lot. She let Faith know that it was hard work and that we had to be intentional about it.

Faith sought the Lord and saw him working in her life. Finally in January, Faith came to our apartment because she decided to commit her life to Christ. Our family prayed with her, but she hesitated to pray. She asked, "Will he understand me?" She was so excited when we told her that God spoke Chinese. She'd never thought of that. We spent about five months discipling her before our departure.

Later that year, when we got back home, we received an e-mail:

Hi, my husband will be baptized this Sunday morning. We prayed nearly every day for it. He is a little different than before. And our life changed a little. Everyday we will take some time to read Bible and study together. I can feel the calmness in our hearts. What a thing. I can also feel I was changed. I don't care the things I chased before that much. Position, money, pride are not as interesting as before to me. But at the same time I feel a little aimless. I don't know what to do next. I should pray. Miss you. All our love, Faith

I received another e-mail three weeks later:

Hi, last Sunday morning my husband received the ceremony of baptism. Before the ceremony began, we sang a lot hymns, and he and other newly believers gave their testimonies. He gave his testimony at the beginning. He said he saw the love in your family, changes in me, and the wisdom of the good book. He said a long time ago he couldn't understand why a Christian will give the enemy his right cheek after his left cheek was slapped. He thought that was stupid. Now he knows that this is not stupid, because a Christian has love in his heart, so he will do this "stupid thing." We all are encouraged by his words. Now he begins to read the Bible very often. What a thing. How great His power is! All my love, Faith.

TERI'S TURN

Olga was a computer science major and my best student. Her English was better than anyone's in the class. She did all the homework, never missed class and always came prepared. She answered questions, worked hard to understand the nuances of the language and did extra readings. Every day she had new vocabulary questions. She loved English and learning.

Olga's class was my last of the day. I usually headed home when it was over. Sometimes Olga would ask if she could ride the train with me. We would ride together, talking nonstop. I would get off at my station, and then she would cross the platform and catch the train back to campus. Occasionally, if we both had time, we'd have tea and a small meal together.

Olga and I enjoyed our hour-long train rides home. We discussed boys, why I had never married, parents and my religion. Olga had many questions about God. Does God exist? How does one know him? Do you believe in the Bible? Do you believe in Jesus? How could Jesus be born of a virgin? Is there life in outer space? (Err . . . what?) Do you have a Bible I can borrow?

Olga was so ready to receive Jesus that I was merely an observer of what God was doing in her life. She told me that when she was very little, her grandmother took care of her while her parents both worked long hours as aeronautical engineers in Ukraine. At night, her grandmother would tuck her in bed and whisper in her ear, "Olga, do not believe what they tell you at school; there is a God. He *does* exist."

In October of that first fall in Moscow, Little Olga, as I affectionately called her, gave her heart to Christ. I had the privilege of watching the experience. Her sweet, round face was filled with light, peace and joy. She thanked God again and again as tears ran down her face. She cried, "I knew it! I knew all the time that he was real!"

Olga met with me regularly for Bible study, and she attended church with me at the Moscow Protestant Chaplaincy. The chaplain there saw that I was bringing several students from my classes to church, so he suggested that he start a student group in his home to explain the foundational beliefs of Christianity. Olga grew in Christ in a way I have never seen before or since. She came to me weekly to discuss what she had learned in that week's foundations class. She was memorizing Scripture, both in English and Russian. She wanted books, commentaries, dictionaries, anything I could get my hands on that would help her learn more about God.

Her life was transformed. Without my lecturing her or telling her about God's laws, one by one she began to let go of the strongholds in her life. She stopped smoking, she gave up alcohol, she stopped sleeping with her boyfriend (he broke up with her). She changed. Olga started having Bible studies in her dorm, six each week, to explain what she had learned about Jesus and why she believed in the Bible.

When Olga graduated from university, the Moscow Protestant Chaplaincy hired her to work full time as the church secretary. This job involved preparing all the materials for the church's activities, taking care of the expatriate pastor and his family, paying bills and organizing events. It is one of the most important jobs in the church.

My parents offered Little Olga a full-ride scholarship to come and study at the seminary of her choice in the U.S. This offer came at a time when Russians were doing anything to get out of the country. Olga graciously refused their offer. "If I go, who will do my job?" she asked. "Who will lead the Bible studies in the dorm? No, thank you. I am doing what God wants me to do right here."

Little Olga is married now. She has two kids. She still works for the church. When my husband and I visited Moscow, the new pastor at the chaplaincy said that he had never seen an individual whose faith so informed her life as did Olga's. She is an incredible person. Lives in Moscow have been changed because of her.

When I went to Russia I was just an old-maid missionary tent-maker with a heart to love my students, trying to make a difference because of all that Christ had done for me. I loved Russia because God loved Russia. I taught English there because that's what I do and that's what the Russians wanted. I met Little Olga because I was her teacher. And now Little Olga is reaching her nation for Christ.

You and I are not Russia's future. Olga is. Mike's not China's future. Faith is. And when we cross a border to teach in a distant classroom we are looking into the future of that nation in each and every student's eyes. They are the future leaders, teachers, parents, engineers, lawyers, government workers. What takes place in that classroom has the potential of transforming an entire society one student at a time.

Crossing borders to teach in a distant classroom can be the most surprising, challenging, difficult and rewarding experience life has to offer. We wouldn't have missed it for the world.

Appendix A
Lesson Plan Template

Date: August 1 2009

Course Title/Class: Example: Intro to Writing [State the time you have in this class] (90 minutes)

I. Greet students/gather up homework/give a starter. (10 minutes)

II. Discuss last week's lesson (review) and how it ties into this week's. State today's objective. (15 minutes)

III. Lecture. Give the title. If you have handouts, give them right before the lecture. (15-20 minutes)

IV. Lecture ends: time for Q & A. Ask questions you have prepared ahead of time. (15 minutes)

V. Have students break into small groups to solve a problem or discuss lecture points. Walk around room and listen to their group discussion without entering into the discussion. (15-20 minutes)

VI. Regather. State something positive: "Good discussions going on. I heard some interesting concepts just now." Remind students of homework and due dates (write these on the board). (5 minutes)

VII. Closure: Any questions, comments? "Okay, write down one thing you learned from today's lesson, one thing you already knew and one thing you wish you knew about this topic." (5 minutes)

VIII. Dismiss.

Websites for Lesson Planning
http://www.eduref.org/Virtual/Lessons/Guide.shtml
http://www.lessonplanspage.com/WriteLessonPlan.htm
http://www.emunix.emich.edu/~jblock/docs/lessonplan.pdf

Appendix B
Course Syllabus Template

UNIVERSITY OR COLLEGE NAME
Course Number and Name
Semester and Year (e.g., Fall 2004)

INSTRUCTOR INFORMATION

Name: Mailbox/Office#:
Office Telephone: Cell Telephone:
E-Mail Address: Office Hours:

COURSE DESCRIPTION:
This course focuses . . . The last part of the course will focus on . . .
This course is required for all . . . and fulfills the requirements for a
degree in . . .

COURSE INFORMATION:
Credit Hours: 3
Prerequisites:
Textbooks:
Supplies Needed:

Recommendation: When setting goals for this course, the successful
student will attend class regularly, prepare assignments well and turn
them in on time, contribute to in-class discussions and group work,
and meet with the instructor at least once during office hours.

COURSE OBJECTIVES:
Upon completion of this course students should be able to:
1.
2.
3.

CONTENT OUTLINE AND COMPETENCIES:

Apply . . . .
Use . . .
Demonstrate . . .

Learn how to
1.
2.
3.
Develop
1.
2.
3.
Express
1.
2.
3.
Recognize
1.
2.
3.

COURSE REQUIREMENTS:

Papers—

Preparation of Papers—Type and double-space all final versions . . .

Late Work—Present all work in class, in person, and on time, except in cases of emergency. **If a major writing assignment is turned in late, ten points will be deducted** . . .

Attendance—required . . . absences . . .

<u>Please Note:</u> a student's grade will be dropped one letter grade as a result of four absences. Six absences and the student will be dropped from class.

Participation—You are expected to be an active participant . . .

Classroom Behavior—Students are asked . . . **cell phones must be turned off during class.**

Quizzes—

Plagiarism—Plagiarism is the act of representing . . . Plagiarism is not accepted.

Tests—

EVALUATION

Table 7

Assignment	Your Points	Points Possible	% of Total Grade
WRITTEN ASSIGNMENTS			
Assignment #1		100	10
Assignment #2		100	10
Assignment #3		100	10
Essay on . . .		100	10
Midterm		100	10
Project		100	10
Subtotals		650	70%
ADDITIONAL WORK			
Class Participation (up to 88 points)		88	8
Quizzes (10 @ 10 points each)		100	10
Final		50	5
Subtotals		350	35%
Totals		1000	100%

Grading Scale
A = 90-100%   B = 80-89%   C = 70-79%   D = 60-69%   F = below 59%

CLASS SCHEDULE

To receive credit for your work, hand in all assignments to the instructor **in person and on time**. If changes in this schedule become necessary, you will be informed in class in advance of the due dates whenever possible. It is advisable to write down all announcements made during the first 5 minutes of class. Reading assignments are from [textbook name].

Week 1

    January 22   LECTURE TITLE:

    HOMEWORK:

Week 2

    January 27   TOPIC:

    HOMEWORK:

    DUE:

Appendix C

Teaching Methods and Learning Styles

(Adapted from Howard Gardner's theory of multiple intelligences. See his Frames of Mind: The Theory of Multiple Intelligences *and* Multiple Intelligences: The Theory in Practice: A Reader.*)*

VISUAL/SPATIAL INTELLIGENCE

Ability to perceive the visual. These learners tend to think in pictures and need to create vivid mental images to retain information. They enjoy looking at maps, charts, pictures, videos and movies.

Skills include puzzle building, reading, writing, understanding charts and graphs, a good sense of direction, sketching, painting, creating visual metaphors and analogies (perhaps through the visual arts), manipulating images, constructing, fixing, designing practical objects, interpreting visual images

Possible career paths: navigators, sculptors, visual artists, inventors, architects, interior designers, mechanics, engineers

VERBAL/LINGUISTIC INTELLIGENCE

Ability to use words and language. These learners have highly developed auditory skills and are generally elegant speakers. They think in words rather than pictures.

Skills include listening, speaking, writing, storytelling, explaining, teaching, using humor, understanding the syntax and meaning of words, remembering information, convincing someone of their point of view, analyzing language usage

Possible career paths: poet, journalist, writer, teacher, lawyer, politician, translator

LOGICAL/MATHEMATICAL INTELLIGENCE

Ability to use reason, logic and numbers. These learners think conceptually in logical and numerical patterns, making connections between pieces of information. Always curious about the world around them, these learners ask lots of questions and like to do experiments.

Skills include problem solving, classifying and categorizing information, working with abstract concepts to figure out the relationship of each to the other, handling long chains of reason to make local progressions, doing controlled experiments, questioning and wondering about natural events, performing complex mathematical calculations, working with geometric shapes

Possible career paths: scientists, engineers, computer programmers, researchers, accountants, mathematicians

BODILY/KINESTHETIC INTELLIGENCE

Ability to control body movements and handle objects skillfully. These learners express themselves through movement. They have a good sense of balance and eye-hand coordination (e.g., ball play, balance beams). Through interacting with the space around them, they are able to remember and process information. `

Skills include dancing, physical coordination, sports, hands-on experimentation, using body language, crafts, acting, miming, using their hands to create or build, expressing emotions through the body

Possible career paths: athletes, physical education teachers, dancers, actors, firefighters, artisans

MUSICAL/RHYTHMIC INTELLIGENCE

Ability to produce and appreciate music. These musically inclined learners think in sounds, rhythms and patterns. They immediately respond to music, either appreciating or criticizing what they hear. Many of these learners are extremely sensitive to environmental sounds (e.g., crickets, bells, dripping taps).

Skills include singing, whistling, playing musical instruments, recognizing tonal patterns, composing music, remembering melodies, understanding the structure and rhythm of music

Possible career paths: musician, disc jockey, singer, composer

INTERPERSONAL INTELLIGENCE

Ability to relate to and understand others. These· learners try to see things from other people's points of view in order to understand how they think and feel. They often have an uncanny ability to sense feelings, intentions and motivations. They are great organizers, although they sometimes resort to manipulation. Generally they try to maintain peace in group settings and encourage cooperation. They use both verbal (speaking) and nonverbal language (e.g., eye contact, body language) to open communication channels with others.

Skills include seeing things from other perspectives (dual-perspective), listening, using empathy, understanding other people's moods and feelings, counseling, cooperating with groups, noticing people's motivations and intentions, communicating both verbally and nonverbally, building trust, peaceful conflict resolution, establishing positive relations with other people

Possible career paths: counselor, salesperson, politician, business person

INTRAPERSONAL INTELLIGENCE

Ability to self-reflect and be aware of one's inner state of being. These learners try to understand their inner feelings, dreams, relationships with others, and strengths and weaknesses.

Skills include recognizing their own strengths and weaknesses, reflecting and analyzing themselves, awareness of their inner feelings, desires and dreams, evaluating their thinking patterns, reasoning with themselves, understanding their role in relationship to others

Possible career paths: researchers, theorists, philosophers

Dedication and Acknowledgments

MICHAEL'S

To Janet, Claire, Max, Spencer and Molly who vigorously embraced the Great Commission and became excellent border-crossers. Thanks for your love, support, willingness to follow God's call to distant lands and endless patience on all of our adventures. May you never lose sight of what God has done in our lives and in the lives of others. Transformation often came through your love and acceptance of those we were called to.

TERI'S

To Daryl, my husband, best friend and colaborer—thanks for asking me to yoke up with your wagon. It's been quite a journey as we've seen God move among the nations. Thanks for always supporting, encouraging, praying and believing. Your banner over me is love. I'm grateful.

❂　❂　❂

We would like to thank first and foremost our families for hanging in there with us as we hammered out this manuscript. Appreciation goes to Al Hsu and all the folks at InterVarsity Press who not only approved our proposal, but worked diligently to present the best book possible. Gratitude goes to all the IICS professors who provided stories and shared their experiences with us. You are the unsung heroes of the faith. Thank you to Dr. Cliff Schimmels's family who allowed us so much access to his materials and insights. He was an excellent educator and border-crosser. He is greatly missed.

We want to acknowledge our good friend Anne Coates who spent long hours proofing the manuscript (even while on vacation) and whose eagle eye brought edits and revisions that were not only needed, but that improved the quality of the work.

Most of all, we would like to acknowledge Dr. Daryl McCarthy with the International Institute for Christian Studies (IICS) whose vision more than twenty years ago has facilitated teachers to answer the call to cross borders and teach in distant classrooms. Lives have been transformed because of your vision and obedience as an administrator and facilitator.

Finally we want to thank the true border-crosser, our Lord Jesus Christ, who provided us with the honor and privilege of teaching in distant classrooms. He alone can transform our hurting and struggling world. You have shown us that you truly do use the foolish things of this world to confound the wise.

Author Index

Subject Index

About the International Institute for Christian Studies

OUR VISION

The IICS vision is that someday every university student in the world will have at least one instructor who will articulate and demonstrate the love and lordship of Jesus Christ for them.

MISSION: Develop Godly Leaders

The Mission of International Institute for Christian Studies is to bring glory to God and impact the world by developing godly leaders for every sector of society—government, business, home, church, the arts, law, the sciences, education—as we provide key universities and academic institutions with educational services and Christian faculty who teach and live in such a way as to draw others to faith and transformation in Christ.

METHOD: Faculty Placement

IICS places faculty from a wide range of disciplines in teaching positions at secular universities outside North America and the UK. We also establish Departments of Christian Studies, provide library collections, sponsor business and teacher training seminars, and provide curriculum consultation.

IMPACT: Knowing Christ

Many students have come to know Christ and have been taught to think and live under his lordship. Outside the classroom, IICS professors are ministering through Bible studies, academic conferences, movie nights, consulting, writing, speaking, evangelism and other settings.

International Institute for Christian Studies (IICS)
P.O. Box 12147
Overland Park, KS 66282-2147
iics@iics.com
http://www.iics.com